MERED1

GETTING
UNSTUCK

A GUIDE TO MOVING YOUR
CAREER FORWARD

ISBN 13: 978-1-63489-468-5

Library of Congress Catalog Number has been applied for.
Printed in the United States of America
First Printing: 2021
25   24   23   22   21   5   4   3   2   1

Cover design by Nupoor Gordon
Interior design by Kim Morehead

Wise Ink Creative Publishing replaces every tree used in printing their books by planting thousands of trees every year in reforestation programs. Learn more at wiseink.com.

This book is dedicated to everyone who believed in me.

Ta-da! We did it.

I'm here to help!
MEREDITH
LEIGH
MODLE

FOREWORD
by Don Thompson

I didn't set out to be the first of anything. Being first wasn't as impactful or as important as being a good person, leveraging a great education, and helping others. This life truth for me was driven through my very essence by my grandmother, Rosa J. Martin. She preached a simple set of values that she embedded in my DNA and reinforced with a life of service grounded in prayer and her unyielding faith in God.

My career has had many shifts; some of those people could see from the outside, and others were driven within me as I have attempted to live a value-based life. In becoming a stronger leader, you will adjust and shift from time to time as you grow, but you must control how and what that shift means to you and others. Developing and living a set of core values that ground you in your purpose can be a tremendous guiding light along life's journeys. These values will help you more clearly understand WHO you are,

WHOSE you are, and WHY you are here—they'll also help you make future decisions that you've never faced before.

When I first met Meredith, she was assisting the writers on the management communications team. When Meredith wrote for me, it felt natural—she understood what I said and how those words and meanings could affect people. As her mentor, I made it a point to explain my actions and why the words were important to building trust and inspiration in a global organization.

As a leader, I understand that my role goes beyond my team, and as an African American leader, my leadership touches far beyond my company or the business community. *To whom much is given, much is required,* but that extra responsibility rides along with intense work weeks, family time, and, yes, time for ourselves. Meredith shares her story of making the difficult decisions and living your values at work. Learning from the lessons in this book will help you better navigate your career. Whether you are just starting your career or you are well along your journey, your impact can be as important as anyone's. Don't get stuck believing you are less than adequate or can't rise to the occasion of your opportunities. Push yourself to become reliably competent in your endeavors, learning more each and every day and surrounding yourself with talented people who enhance your life and share common values of success in life.

It's appropriate Meredith's book is called *Getting Unstuck*, because we often get stuck between the tension of our values and our daily lives pulling us in different directions. We all seek stronger balance in living a full life, and it's fundamentally important to align your purpose with your passion. At McDonald's, I knew my intention wasn't hamburgers alone; it was helping people, and I have been blessed to find places to make an impact doing both. My journey continues today at Cleveland Avenue, LLC, and I hope your journey will continue and be enhanced by Meredith's illuminating guide for a pathway to even more success in your whole life.

> —*Don Thompson, founder and CEO*
> *of Cleveland Avenue and former president*
> *and CEO of McDonald's Corporation*

INTRODUCTION

"An army of sheep led by a lion
can defeat an army of lions led by a sheep."
—*Ghanaian proverb*

Growing up in my predominately white hometown, I learned that being the first doesn't mean you are going to stay the only one. In fifth grade, we elected the first woman and the first African American person as our mayor. Fifteen years later, I watched Barack Obama become the first African American president of the United States of America.

Seeing these pivotal firsts, these moments in history, instilled in me a special pride and responsibility; I knew I wanted to be a leader, and I understood it was rare to see people who looked like me in leadership. As I grew older, I made sure that I smiled and said "hi" to anyone else of

1

color I came across. It was important for people to know I saw them because I expected them to see me. Because of those that came before me, I believed it was possible to be respected and to treat those working with you as though they were just as important as the next person. Throughout my career, I've taken the spirit of my hometown with me, and as a communicator working in diversity, I've seen first-hand the importance of service, mentoring, and communication. These people have inspired me to think differently about my career and my legacy, and I hope my words help inspire you as well.

When I graduated from Howard University with a degree in journalism and African American history, my entrepreneur dad gave me his trademark straightforward advice, which was really more of a demand: "You need to make $50,000 coming out of school." I trusted he knew what he was talking about and started my climb through corporate America in finance.

Like many young people, I recognized my desire for clear communication, strong mentors, and a purposeful, service-focused life as my core strengths, but I struggled to align service and mentoring with a fulfilling corporate career.

For a few years, I suffered through a career that didn't fit. I have a creative personality, and finance . . . well, it just wasn't ready for me. So, at twenty-five, I quit my job for the first time and took an internship at an ad agency in downtown Chicago, making seventeen dollars an hour with no benefits, which was a significant pay cut.

My dad came to visit and told me I needed to make better decisions.

Even though it hurt to hear his judgments, I realized that this advertising position wasn't right either. I didn't like working in an agency, and I *really* didn't like only getting paid seventeen dollars an hour when I was used to more. So I kept looking for new opportunities, and eventually, despite being a vegan, got an interview for—and then landed—a position as a communications supervisor at the McDonald's corporation. Yes, *that* McDonald's.

Working at such a big corporation, I was worried I would feel isolated. Like many of us, I struggle with imposter syndrome, and during my years there I suffered from health challenges ranging from anxiety to temporary blindness. But despite these challenges, at McDonald's I really started to figure out what was important and which values I couldn't drop.

Getting Unstuck isn't just a magical formula that can get you tons of success for none of the stress. It's a guide to understanding how to move you from where you are to where you know you can go and to teach you how you can bring others with you.

In my time in corporate America, I learned from many mentors, got *way* more experience than I bargained for, and decided for myself what I needed to focus on in order to grow. And at the end of it all, I had a set of steps that were a recipe for success—for growth, for vision, for achieving meaningful goals. Together, I call them TRIBE.

TRIBE is a methodology you can use to keep your goals and vision a priority. It is a simple reminder, a structure to protect you from falling into bad habits. At its base level, it's also an acronym:

TIME
RESOURCES
INNOVATION
BELIEF
EVOLUTION

Each component of TRIBE is key to your personal and professional journey. Since writing *Getting Unstuck*, I've successfully led my leadership development and communications company, Leverette Weekes, and served clients around the world. I've also endured COVID-19, divorce, distance learning, and taking responsibility for my life as a single parent. It hasn't been easy; TRIBE has helped me to stay on track, increase my income, and advance my career.

I've heard from clients how making the space to answer the questions in this book has allowed them to clarify what they want and take the steps to change their life. TRIBE's affirmations will help you recognize when something is wrong. It will teach you how to adjust, to stand up for yourself, and to know when it's time to take action. With this framework, I believe you will be able to escape toxic cultures if you can't change them, and navigate your career successfully even in the aftermath of the unprecedented experience that was 2020.

While no one knows the future of work, throughout the book, I will prompt you to check in with yourself. Use these pages to keep track of your thoughts in a single place so you can see your progress and where you are feeling stuck.

For support as you read, sign up for my mailing list by texting UNSTUCK to 66866 if you are in the US or dropping me an email at info@Leveretteweekes.com.

Get a notebook, turn the page; you are about to get unstuck.

GETTING STARTED:
SEE YOURSELF DIFFERENTLY

"Where you sit when you are old shows where you
stood in youth."
—*African proverb*

When I first met Kelly, she had the longest tenure in her department. She was hired straight out of college, before she married or had kids. But, as she got older, everything in her life grew up except her career. Kelly was good at her job, of course, but she wanted a promotion. She applied for professional development programs and positions in other departments and even shadowed leaders to try to break the glass ceiling. She knew all the logistics of her job, like the best way to get corporate to approve a budget overage. She was efficient and detail-oriented, keeping track of all the little things that might slip another employee's mind. But even though her company was struggling to keep top leaders—they hired new managers every six months—Kelly's name never came up for promotion, and all her applications were denied.

Figuring out long term goals

JOURNAL PROMPT:

What challenge am I dealing with right now in my career?

As women in the workplace, we are told anything is possible and that if a woman hasn't done it yet, then we can be the first. But even if we can see the next step, in reality there are still unwritten rules that can make it impossible to reach. Kelly tried to be open to feedback, but no matter how much her performance improved and how much she supported her manager, no one was willing to let her move forward in her career.

During management meetings, Kelly's managers said she was too caught up in office politics. They said she was aggressive, bossy, and too focused on promoting her own brand. They said she wasn't a team player and that she was determined to lead even when it wasn't her place. Finally, they suggested she didn't have the time to improve her management style because of her responsibility at home as a mother of three young kids.

ambiguity ———— Not being good / confident at closing

a gift

What part of my job do I complain the most about?

After nearly ten years in the same role, Kelly was at the end of her rope. She wanted to quit but, like most of us, needed health care and a steady salary. Her youngest child was only six months old, and she couldn't afford a lapse in coverage.

All the reasons Kelly's bosses provided for her lack of a promotion were just excuses. The truth was that she wasn't promoted because she was perfect for her current position. If Kelly moved to another area, her manager's work would be disrupted. Her career was stalled because of her company's apathy and laziness. They didn't promote Kelly because it was convenient for them to keep her in the same place, letting her think it was her lack of ambition or an inability to do her job.

She thought the closed doors and negative feedback meant she was failing, but in reality she was getting to the top of her game. She had developed leadership skills to navigate the turnover of her managers. She liked her coworkers and enjoyed keeping her team motivated while the company looked for new leaders.

Finally, after a long string of bad higher-ups, I was hired

as Kelly's manager, and I recognized that she was trapped. I knew, because I felt that way too.

Before you can meaningfully change your life and your job for the better, you need a good understanding of what isn't working in your current situation.

JOURNAL PROMPT:
How long can I live like this?

We were both workaholics with type A, dominant personalities. We believed in fairness, and we motivated each other by sharing our experiences. The same passion that drew us to careers in philanthropy led us to spend more time on other people's work and responsibilities than our own. This left us feeling tired and underappreciated.

We wanted to save our department. We loved our co-workers and our office space, and we loved working together. But, at the end of the day, we wanted equal pay and advancement, and no one but us was coming to save our careers.

So there we were: me as manager, Kelly as disgruntled employee, both trapped and falling victim to the common pitfalls of women in big organizations. As we walked to the parking lot one day, I asked her if she was happy at work. She kept her eyes focused on her feet and started to tell me that even though she liked working with me, she was still unhappy. Having a better manager helped her to see how she was outgrowing the job. And, in that moment, I realized if I was as unhappy at work as she was, I had to take the advice I wanted to give Kelly and figure out what would make me happy.

We decided to help each other.

A Week of Exploration

The first thing we did was explore. When you're bogged down with surviving a bad day-to-day situation, it's easy to stop dreaming. When that happens, you lose sight of what will make your life better. You have to think differently. To be successful, you have to envision your life in the future.

> "To get lost is to learn the way."
> —*African proverb*

Working with my coaching clients, I've noticed a trend— high-performing leaders are self-aware and constantly checking and adjusting their course. Successful leaders view their role like a captain. Their role is to show up at their best to help guide the crew and passengers to safety. One person can't do it all, and the captain has to navigate the cockpit equipment, weather, and any unforeseeable events that can quickly turn disastrous. Instead of being frustrated by change, a pilot shifts their mind-set to see opportunities and guide themselves in the right direction. By having access to a map, they can more easily judge when they need to speed up, change course, or refuel. After I decided I wasn't happy in my job, I took a week to figure out what it was I really wanted, and I experienced what life would be like when I was truly in charge.

I had to step outside of my career, my achievements, and even my family. For one week, I gave myself time away from everyone else's expectations. I cleared my calendar and got off social media. Before I told anyone about my new plan or what was next, I started by checking in with myself.

I divided my life into six sections so I could see my goals more clearly and assess where I needed to direct my time and energy first.

Each day I meditated on an area of my life:

- finances
- relationships
- spirituality
- education
- career
- health

I tackled one goal per day, coming up with broad,

guiding questions to get me to journal about each topic. In my journal entry, I brainstormed my ideal situation with respect to each day's theme. Then, below that, I wrote down a list of statements I wanted to be true in one year. Instead of focusing on what I did not see and getting dejected, I developed five statements to describe what I wanted in my life.

I didn't set specific, discrete goals. Instead, they were a guide for how I want my life to *feel*. They were rooted in broad, emotional terms but left the door open for unexpected opportunities. I used these statements as a tool that I could always return to if I felt like I needed a push in the right direction. These statements gave me a map that helped me define success for myself.

"Success in life depends largely on how you handle your failures."
—*African proverb*

ACTIVITY 1: YOUR WEEK OF POSSIBILITIES

Write a journal entry about each category below in response to the questions.

Then, write five personal intentions that state your goals as though they are your reality.

Use my statements as inspiration but understand that your goals will be (and should be!) different as you define what success means to you.

No breakdowns, only breakthroughs.

This week is about breaking your rules and letting go of assumptions rooted in limiting beliefs.

MONDAY - FINANCES

Money and finance can be a major source of stress. Today we start with how you feel about money and its role in your transition to getting unstuck. The questions to consider today are about finding the line between needs and hopes. Release your fears and allow yourself to dream big! If you are feeling stuck, try shifting your mindset. Consider what you would do with $100,000; what you would buy first, what debt you would pay off, and how much you would save for retirement? Allow yourself to be free to see your financial future differently than it is today.

Journal Questions:

- *What would it take for me to not worry about money?*
- *What are my needs, and what are my wants?*
- *If I didn't have to worry about money, what would I do with the capital?*
- *What would I do with my time if I didn't have to worry about money?*
- *What is my best-case scenario when it comes to my finances?* NOt being afraid of them
- *What would it take to make my best-case scenario be true?*

↳ Needs bigger savings for house / retirement

↳ wants to travel

Some statements to get you started:

- I am attracting more resources to cover my expenses and save for my future.
- I am confident in my financial plan with goals for home ownership, debt reduction, and wealth transfer.
- I trust my team of advisors to help me navigate my financial goals.

What are your statements?

Actions I will take:

1.
2.
3.

> You must act as if it is impossible to fail.
> — *Ashanti proverb*

TUESDAY - RELATIONSHIPS

Today is about the energy and motivation you have to create and maintain personal connections. Remember: relationships come in all forms. Who would you spend more time with if you had unlimited time and money? If today's assignment feels overwhelming, try mapping your relationships first:

- Who have I seen in person in the last seven days? In the last month? 7days - John, Ciara, O+K, F+L
- Who have I spoken to on the phone? In the last week? In the last month?

Journal Questions:
- *Where do I feel energized and uplifted?*
- *Who is around me when I feel energized and uplifted?*
- *How often am I with my loved ones?*
- *Do I want to grow my circle? In which ways?*
- *In the best-case scenario, what does my family and social circle look like?*
- *What would it take to make my relationships look like my best-case scenario?*

Some statements to get you started:
- I am loved and valued.

- I get positive energy from my personal and professional relationships.
- My relationships add value to my day and energy to my spirit.
- My network supports my goals and encourages me to grow.
- I am present and mindful with others and myself.

What are your statements?

Actions I will take:

1.
2.
3.

> "Show me your friend,
> and I will show you your character."
> —*African proverb*

WEDNESDAY - SPIRITUALITY

Today isn't about your religion, it's about your inner belief in your purpose and role in the greater universe. Connecting with that intention today will help you tap into why you do the things you do and why you value what you do.

Your truth is yours; explore what is true for you.

Journal Questions:
- *How do I improve people's lives?*
- *How am I supporting my community?*
- *How am I being brave?*
- *How do I make an impact? On who?*
- *Do I spend my time supporting others?*
- *Do I spend my time supporting myself?*
- *What do I believe in?*
- *What would it take for me to feel the best about how I'm living and connecting to the world around me?*

Some statements to get you started:
- I have enough time and space to support my spiritual routines (meditation, prayer, reflection time). I am not overscheduled or exhausted.
- My daily schedule is aligned with my beliefs at work and at home.

- I help others daily.
- I know how to connect with my higher power.
- I see miracles in my life.

What are your statements?

Actions I will take:

1.
2.
3.

> "The fool speaks, the wise man listens."
> —*Ethiopian proverb*

THURSDAY - EDUCATION

Today, consider what you've learned so far in your life, but don't limit yourself to just formal education or degrees. Life lessons from business, navigating transitions, and family life apply here too! Now, think about how you want to grow. For many of us, education is the single most important thing that expands our opportunities and challenges others to see our value.

Journal Questions:
- *How am I expanding my knowledge?*
- *How am I challenging myself?*
- *What is the next milestone in my education?*
- *What lesson am I learning?*
- *What topics interest me?*

Some statements to get you started:
- I read and write daily. I am actively learning and improving my skills.
- I am motivated to learn. I have a timeline for my next certification, degree, or examination.
- I am becoming the person I want to be.
- My education satisfies my curiosity. I am pursuing topics that interest me and move me forward.

- I feel challenged and engaged. I am inspired, and my time feels well spent learning.

What are your statements?

Actions I will take:
1.
2.
3.

"Instruction in youth is like engraving in stone."
—*Moroccan proverb*

FRIDAY - CAREER

Today, focus on your future, not your current career. If you believed that your career goals will come true, what would you do differently today? Tomorrow's careers haven't been invented yet, so dream big and explore.

Journal Questions:
- *Where am I spending my time?*
- *How much am I worth?*
- *What are my professional goals?*
- *If education and experience were not a barrier, what would I like more of in my work life?*
- *Why did I apply for or accept my current (or most recent) role?*
- *Where can I focus my energy if I'm in need of a transition?*
- *Where will my business take me?*

Some statements to get you started:
- I am passionate about my work. I want to go early and stay late.
- I am focused on my purpose and using my gifts.
- I am in a psychologically safe and healthy environment. I am not manipulated, harassed, or harmed in my workplace.

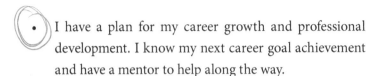
- I have a plan for my career growth and professional development. I know my next career goal achievement and have a mentor to help along the way.
- I believe my daily job helps people and improves the world.

What are your statements?

Actions I will take:
1.
2.
3.

"Wisdom is not like money to be tied up and hidden."
—Akan proverb

SATURDAY - HEALTH

You made it through the traditional work week, so spend this weekend checking in with you. Graveyards are full of men and women with big dreams but no health—what will you be able to do if you take care of yourself?

In a lot of ways, this is the most difficult topic to consider. It's always painful to realize that you can't do it all, so really take the time to reflect on your responses. Are you surprised by any of your answers? Today is about aligning your mind and body—what questions are you afraid to ask? Where do you need to make a space so you can keep yourself healthy and keep yourself aligned with the previous days' statements?

Journal Questions:
- *Do I have enough energy to complete what is expected of me?*
- *What is the easiest thing I could do for myself to improve my health?*
- *Do I make health a priority? How so?*
- *What do I put before my health?*
- *If I had no limits on my time or resources, what would I be doing to take care of myself?*
- *What steps can I take to make my best-case scenario a reality?*

Some statements to get you started:

- My body, mind, and soul are in perfect health.
- I have scheduled my doctor's appointments and am proactively addressing all physical and mental needs.
- I have resources for my mental, physical, and spiritual health.
- I am confident in my appearance. My hair, attire, and brand match my personal and professional goals.
- I feel safe and secure at work and at home.
- I am able to sleep for 7–8 hours each night.
- I have a stress management routine for my body. I take time for a massage, haircut, manicure/pedicure, and facial monthly. I make time to stretch, move my body, and break a sweat.
- I honor my body with my food and beverage choices. I eat whole grains, drink water instead of pop, and avoid sugar.

What are your statements?

Actions I will take:

1.
2.
3.

> "If you close your eyes to facts,
> you will learn through accidents."
> —*African proverb*

SUNDAY – INSPIRATION

Congratulations! You've almost made it through your week of possibilities. Now it's time to reflect on the positive work you've done for the past six days. Use Sunday to write down statements that inspire you.

Maybe you have a quote or an affirmation that speaks to you. If not, write your own. Tap into the inspiration and passion you have, because you'll need that motivation to get unstuck.

Here's mine: I am already perfect and prepared.

Actions I will take:
1.
2.
3.

TIME

The only asset you can never control is time.

We just spent a whole week envisioning a better future where time was of no consequence to your dreams, but back in reality, your current life will always present challenges that seem impossible to escape. There are many work environments that don't allow their employees the time to dream, grow, or even take care of themselves and their families.

You need to notice where you have lost control of your time and take it back for yourself.

Kelly was a mother, and with that joy comes great responsibility. She wanted to care for her children, have a strong relationship with them, and attend school and church events with her family. The rest of the employees in her department worked until around seven o'clock and then went to happy hour. At these happy hours, the other employees criticized Kelly for her "mismatched priorities." They judged her for not coming out with them and took it personally instead of realizing that her time with her children was more important to her than happy hour. Since she never spent time with them outside of work, they thought that she was not a team player, though her work in the office demonstrated otherwise. She never got to cultivate strong relationships with her peers and hiring managers, because in that specific office culture, those relationships were made at happy hour. Since her higher-ups didn't feel personally connected to her, they never considered her for a promotion.

Watch out: Unfortunately, many corporate cultures are not accommodating of life outside of work, forcing employees to work overtime both at their jobs and in their family responsibilities. I felt, and continue to feel, for Kelly. She wasn't the only one who was under constant scrutiny from her peers for her attempts to balance her life and career.

When I started my career in finance, I learned to hate early morning conference calls (as I hate anything that starts before 10:00 a.m.). As I advanced in my career, I saw more people work from home and use technology to bridge the gap between their demanding careers and personal lives. Though working from home is a convenient option, it can create awkward scenarios when you are faced with home and work responsibilities at the same time.

When our son was only a few weeks old, I believed I could balance being both the perfect mom and the perfect boss. A few weeks after my maternity leave ended, I sat on his bedroom floor to watch him sleep. I gently shifted my laptop and dialed in to a big conference call, patiently waiting for my name to be called. As I waited for everyone to join, I heard a baby crying in my headphones. I hit the mute button as a message popped up in my email. "Meredith, please mute your line—we can all hear your child."

I was stunned and indignant (my baby was asleep!), but mostly, I was embarrassed. I quickly responded, noticing that the moderator had copied every person on the call in that message to me. I already felt guilty and wanted to prove my commitment, so I stayed up until midnight catching up on emails while I helped my baby get to sleep.

For years, I searched for parenting resources to help me stay in my high-demand career while building a relationship with our sons. I spent all my time worrying about my job. I felt pressure from my company to change my parenting style, marriage, and values to be a better employee, but I only felt like a worse version of myself.

I wasn't being authentic, and I felt trapped.

After only a few weeks of balancing motherhood and my career, I grew tired of explaining sick kids, early pickups, and sleepless nights. I felt like the only person who had a family outside of work.

I worked nonstop and started to feel bad about missing networking opportunities because of lack of childcare. I felt just like Kelly had felt, and I didn't want my coworkers to think I was avoiding them. Yet, I also resented the time I spent at work because every day, my job asked me to find ways to manage my children quietly without disrupting others with my "issues."

**Every time I mentioned my kids,
I felt judged for not being able to control
the most uncontrollable element of life: other people.**

Every day as parents, we wake up early and stay up late. We try to avoid the "bad image" of our kid's problems surprising us at work by managing our workload outside of business hours. The question I was afraid to ask was, "Is this normal?" I didn't know what I would do if someone said it wasn't, and I couldn't handle it if someone told me my life wouldn't get better. Instead, I avoided the question and let valuable opportunities for advice and potential jobs pass me by because I was afraid to share my frustration.

As a woman, the transition to becoming a mom at work made me feel like I was always failing. Either I was too "career" to be a wife and mom or too busy taking care of my kids to be serious at work. My peers made judgmental comments to me about how I balanced my ambition and life goals. The comments ranged from calling me a bad mom to asking me when I had time to see my husband. My peers created a work environment where I felt guilty every time I had a personal obligation, even if it was necessary.

JOURNAL PROMPT:

In what ways am I causing myself to be overwhelmed by the tension between my values and my time?

The Breaking Point

In the spring of 2013, I was throwing up five or six times a day, and my husband (at the time) and I started to worry. We found out we were pregnant, but even then the doctor couldn't explain my nausea or my unexpected bleeding. During our second visit, I read my chart over the nurse's shoulder. *Threatened abortion* was written next to my name. My heart stopped, and I held my breath. The doctor showed us the ultrasound and told us we should come back for weekly monitoring to see *if* the embryo developed. I remember resenting the use of "if" before breaking into tears as I walked to the parking lot. When we got home, I went to my room and prayed to every ancestor to protect this baby.

My nausea and vomiting continued. At this point in my career, I was a director of global community engagement for McDonald's, so I often had to travel to build international relationships. I had an important trip to Brazil scheduled. The company wanted to invest in educational training for young people and people with disabilities who lived in a *favela* (a shanty town), so they would have viable career options when they grew older rather than being forced into illegal activities. I knew it was an important project and that my company was counting on me, so despite the doctor's warning about traveling internationally, I ignored that I was feeling faint and boarded the six-hour flight to São Paulo.

Several hours into the flight, my legs felt wet. I prayed quietly as I got up from my seat, went to the bathroom, and closed the door. Sure enough, I saw blood as I pulled my underwear down.

I was sixteen weeks pregnant and bleeding in the bathroom on a six-hour flight to Brazil.

There was nothing anyone could do so I gave it all up to God. We landed safely, and twenty-four hours later I was still bleeding and throwing up in my hotel room. As I completed all my work obligations, dripping blood the whole time, all I thought about was that the company had paid for me to come down here and do a job. I was not going to let them down.

A few weeks after returning home, I was scheduled to leave for Europe. Two days before my departure, my husband sat me down. He said that traveling internationally in my condition wasn't safe—I had a high-risk pregnancy, and no job was worth going against medical advice. We agreed it was time to make a change. I would have to tell my boss that I was pregnant and couldn't travel.

It's one thing to tell your boss about your personal medical complications; it's another thing when you are leading a department. Word spread that I was pulling back at work and I started getting left out of calls. I got tired of fighting to be heard. I realized that my work culture didn't allow me to care for my health. How would I manage motherhood and marriage if I couldn't find the space to care for my pregnant self?

Things came to a head a year and a half later when our son was approaching his first birthday. I was excited to celebrate with our friends and family. We'd planned a day at the museum, and I was daydreaming about the moment where I could snuggle up with him for cake and ice cream. But then, a week before the big day, I noticed an appointment pop up on my calendar. It ran from seven o'clock in the morning to five o'clock at night on my son's birthday.

Tears welled up in my eyes at the idea of missing the whole day with my son. He would never turn one again, and as his mom I couldn't imagine only experiencing the day through pictures. Any other time I would have cleared my personal schedule for my work obligations, but his first birthday was a special milestone for me. I wanted to celebrate one year of serving as a mother and recovering from a terrible pregnancy and a C-section. I also just needed a break.

I decided to decline the meeting. I was worried how my boss would respond, and how I would handle the situation if he told me that I absolutely had to work.

During our weekly check-in, I explained to him that I had worked twelve- to fourteen-hour days lately and was really looking forward to celebrating my personal milestone as a parent. My boss responded that he was glad I was creating the kind of career environment that would allow me to honor my son's birthday. He told me he'd missed many of his children's milestones, and rattled off all the graduations, plays, performances, and games he'd watched while fielding conference calls or reviewing emails. It wasn't the first time one of my managers had shared their journey, but this time felt different.

I knew right away that I wanted to live my life my way, not to advise others to learn from my mistakes. Making time for my son's first birthday was a victory. I value being fully present in my work, whether I am at home or in the office—I do not see the value in constantly trying to do both at the same time. I knew I had a choice: I could either invest my full time into my corporate employer, or I could try something different and invest in my personal plan for my life beyond my career.

Honoring Your Time

If it costs you your peace, it's too expensive. You are the only one who can be there for your son's birthday. You are the only one who can write your resume or contact a recruiter for a different job. You are the only one who can make sure that you get enough sleep at night so you're not too exhausted to work.

> **Take responsibility for your time and take action in the moment. If you don't pay attention, you will end up giving away all your time for free.**

When I took the day off for my son's birthday, I was taking charge of my time, but it was important to me that it wasn't just a one-off victory. Instead, I began to do some research into how I could make this lasting change, and it helped me feel unstuck.

I spent a few weeks researching how other executives balanced the daily demands of leadership with their home life. I picked people who had similar backgrounds and responsibilities as me—I wanted to know how they personally managed their time and understand how their corporate cultures handled family structure. Furthermore, I asked my existing network to help me save time by pre-screening leaders to interview; my network was familiar with my work style and could give me direct feedback on new types of company cultures I should look into during my research.

Tips for interviewing:
- Do: ask people you trust.
- Do: research and have prepared questions.
- Do: ask how you can support their goals.
- Don't: ask to pick their brain or hide your intentions.
- Don't: ask to be mentored, sponsored, or advised.
- Don't: expect anyone to care about your work, life, or quest for balance as much as you do.

My interviews didn't take too long, but talking to leaders in my same situation as they navigated company cultures that better fit my goals helped build my confidence, and gave me a better understanding of what to look for when reviewing new opportunities. I didn't need an executive search consultant or even a paid membership on LinkedIn.

All I needed was the curiosity to learn more about where I wanted to work and what I needed to achieve my goals.

I realized that there were many other companies that would treat my time with respect and allow me to have a healthy relationship with myself and with my family. My short-term activity allowed me to make a big-picture change: I quit my job.

After I quit, I started to notice all the ways that my job had triggered my feelings and thoughts of inadequacy. I felt like I was not worthy of a promotion because my work told me that my family got in the way of my productivity, even though I worked constantly. They made me feel as though I had to give them every last bit of my time to meet the minimum performance requirements. I realized how much shame my job had imposed on my life.

After I located the source of my stress, it changed how I handled my new position. I had more patience during the afternoon drive home with my kids and in the evening with my family. I stopped taking out my frustrations at home because work no longer made me feel bad about myself every day. When I changed my environment, it changed everything.

If you communicate your needs to your organization and feel like you aren't being heard, then maybe it is time for a change. We all want to push ourselves to do our best work, but we should be mindful to never compromise our health and values. Change starts with awareness of your current situation. Be honest with yourself. Remember that you are the only person who can identify what you need.

Company cultures range from inspiring to damaging, and what works for one person might be terrible for another.

To really assess whether you fit into a culture, you have to be willing to get to know it.

It's important to realize that job changes are not a waste of time, but opportunities to learn more about what you're looking for—the only way for you to figure out what work culture is the best fit for you is to expose yourself to many of them. With each experience, your future goals and opportunities will shift.

Be honest about what you need at this point in your career. I learned more from my mistakes (remember that advertising job in Chicago?) than the decisions I made right the first time; managing life's unpredictable gifts will make you a more empathetic, creative, and interesting person.

Striking a Balance

Not everyone goes into the office to work. If you are spending forty or even eighty hours a week at a job, it might seem like you deserve to spend some time on personal needs during work, and in a lot of cases, it's true; but as a reminder and a word of caution, know that your time is important. No one wants to be like Carl.

For two weeks, I watched Carl come to work early and leave late. Each morning he would stop into my office with an update on his "big project" work. He would linger around the coffee bar and share a fun fact with the highest-ranking executive on the floor. This camaraderie made him likable and memorable—in passing, executives would ask what Carl was working on, and they'd mention his insightful fun facts during small talk with me. Other departments described him as a critical partner and great ambassador. Every time he got something right, it was labeled a game-changer.

Carl was always requested to be the department liaison despite his lamentable work ethic. His coworkers never knew where he was or what he was working on. Despite his always being present, his team could never talk about his impact or what he did. He was good at being at the right place, but no one could tell me why he was there, or what all his alleged hard work was going toward, despite the fact that he was in the office at all times.

But then I noticed a pattern.

I found out that Carl had a deal with other male

employees to "check each other in" at 8:00 a.m. They noticed how higher-ups would survey offices and wanted to give the impression of always burning the midnight oil. Whoever arrived at work first would turn on the other person's computer and lights and leave coffee on their desk. This bro code excluded the rest of Carl's female coworkers.

Carl's bro-code scheme was not a good idea for a number of reasons, but chief among them was that it wasn't sustainable. Having a coworker make you look present can quickly backfire if your boss calls a surprise meeting, decides to wait in your office, or declares an emergency. And eventually, higher-ups will realize that even though you're "present" all the time, not much is actually getting accomplished, and you'll be seen as unproductive.

Instead of creating an elaborate work-life persona, be honest about your ideal work hours. Faking it won't help you make it if you can't cut the hours. It's better to know early if you can't wake up in time for your job.

Once you admit you have a time management problem, you and your higher-ups can take steps to deal with it and figure out a schedule that will hopefully balance your needs with the company's. If you continue outright *wasting* company time to accommodate your schedule, that's good for no one. Not only are you stunting your ability to manage time effectively, you become a huge time drain for your coworkers, inflicting the same pain on them that you've found yourself suffering.

Stay Above the Clouds

There is one mentor in my life who has made an impression on me as someone who strives to align his time with his values. Don Thompson, CEO and founder of Cleveland Avenue and one of the few African Americans ever to lead a Fortune 500 company, made sure vital dates for his family were honored on his calendar. From birthdays to sports games, he showed me how to balance work and family and how to be a parent as well as a high-performing professional. Before every meal in every environment on every continent, I saw him make time to call home and pause to pray. He invited me into his family as a young worker and adopted me as a mentee, sponsor, and a friend. I learned too many lessons to name from having the opportunity to work alongside a leader of Mr. Thompson's caliber, but the most valuable was that he demonstrated that there is always time for your values, because *you* are in control of your time.

With the incredibly heavy demands on his time that come with being an executive, Don was often asked how he prioritized. His response was a simple list: "God, me, and my family." This one sentence reminded him why he was going to work and impacted how he saw his role.

It's one thing to stick to your values as an everyday practice; it's another to do so during times of extreme stress. Even in difficult situations, Mr. Thompson kept his values at the forefront of his mind. One time, I was sitting across from him and my manager, Pat Harris, on a return trip from an Executive Leadership Council gala in the McDonald's jet. Our flight was caught in a severe thunderstorm—alarms were going off, and I swear I heard the pilot cuss over the PA. But all the leaders on the plane were calm. They each prayed quietly and kept chatting like nothing was happening.

I was in shock, trying not to cry. I could feel my fear taking over just as Mr. Thompson gently told me, "It will get better when we get above the clouds." This was true for both plane turbulence and as a larger metaphor for leadership. There were no steps I could take to make the experience better other than calming myself and riding it out, ignoring all the little bumps along the way in favor of focusing on the end goal. At that moment he comforted me, encouraged me, and showed me what a leader is supposed to do in uncertain times.

When our lives are turbulent and we're stuck in our own thunderstorms, it is easy to stick to our daily routines and feel overwhelmed by shame and confusion, sacrificing our time to things we don't believe in because we can't see any other option.

In order to break patterns, we must pay close attention to what those patterns are. We need to assess the demands on our time and take some action in the moment, however small, to change our trajectory. Don't get lost in distractions—get above the clouds.

"If you can't resolve your problems in peace,
you can't solve them in war."
—*Somali proverb*

ACTIVITY 2: CLAIMING YOUR TIME

Where in your life do you need a shift? This activity will help you identify the places where you're losing time by focusing on things you can't control.

STEP 1:

Start by reviewing your calendar from last week and select three colors to color-code your activities and events.

Green: I did this
Yellow: I missed this
Red: This was unrealistic

Ask yourself: What was the best thing about that?

STEP 2:

Spend a week reviewing your schedule at the end of every day. Examine all your activities and obligations. Every day, write a journal entry in response to these questions:

Ask yourself:

- Is there a pattern of things I missed?
- Are there some things I'm just not committed to

doing that are just keeping me overscheduled and feeling guilty?

- Where can I say no to avoid overcommitting myself?

Five tips if you are feeling stuck:

1. Check your social—unfollow what doesn't inspire you and encourage you to think positively. Follow @meredithleighmoore on Instagram and LinkedIn to connect with me.

2. Declutter your real and digital life—organize your inbox and phone so you can stop wading through information you don't need.

3. Switch up your circle—try spending time with new people and new hobbies if the regular routine isn't giving you joy anymore.

4. Change your environment—if you can't go out of town, get a new perspective visiting art galleries, museums, or a new artist's performance.

5. Get a fresh start—cleanse and declutter your system by focusing on your health. Set a goal to eat five fruits and vegetables a day and drink eight glasses of water.

Actions I will take:

1.
2.
3.

STEP 3:

Spend the next week considering the questions that corresponds to that day. Compare them to the positive statements below and pick something small you can do to help you get unstuck and take control of your time.

Monday:

Think about the last time you let someone else control your time. How did it feel?

Affirmations:

- I am the master of my time.
- I will honor my priorities with my time.
- I will set healthy boundaries and say no at the right times for me.
- I will not wait for today to be good, I will make today great.

Tuesday:

Identify areas of your life where you feel you have lost ownership.

Affirmations:

- I am excited to pay attention to the details of my life.
- In order to manage my time well, I have to own every area of my life.
- I will trust my intuition about the relationships that nurture me and encourage my growth.
- I will not let anything, whether it's people or responsibilities, take the most important aspects of my life away from me.

Wednesday:

What are your priorities based on your current actions? How do those priorities align with the priorities you wish you acted on?

Affirmations:

- If I wish to be truly effective, I must know what I want.
- I am what I want and I attract what I am.
- If my personal priorities fundamentally don't align with my career priorities, something has to give.

Thursday:

If you don't value your time, no one will. Are you ready to start taking responsibility for your time?

Affirmations:

- I will release the habits blocking my blessings.
- Today is a beautiful day, there won't be another like it.
- Only I can take responsibility for my time; if I trust it to other people, it will be misused.

Friday:

It is important to know not only what your priorities are but why you hold them. What would happen if you didn't control your time?

Affirmations:
- I am purposefully living my best life.
- I am claiming victory and peace. I see today is a great day for me.

Saturday and Sunday:

Think about the last twenty-four hours. List how you spent your time and place an x next to the items that are in line with your vision for your future. What tasks helped you be productive? What people in your life have helped you?

Affirmations:
- I accept myself unconditionally. I accept I have strengths and weaknesses.
- I will devote myself to living my time on my terms.

- I will find a harmony between my career and my personal life, making sure I stay ahead in the workplace while giving what I love the time it deserves.
- I will focus on tasks that encourage my productivity and jettison activities that are a drain on my time.
- I will surround myself with people who help me to use my time in the best way possible.

Tips to manage your time:
- Create a ninety-minute playlist to remind you to take a break once it ends. Include the sounds of calming ocean waves to help you stay calm and practice deep breathing.
- Sign up for a service like Shine Text that sends you daily inspirational and encouraging messages.
- Pick a theme song to celebrate when you honor your time. Mine is "I Am Moana" because if I could be anything I would be a Disney princess.

STEP 4:

Now, it's time to create a skeleton schedule that will keep you in control of your time and keep your days aligned with your values. Block out your day and try to stick to it. There will always be days where every schedule is thrown out the window, but it's good to have a baseline to return to.

Here's a sample of my daily schedule:

5:00–6:00 a.m.	Meditation, personal time
6:00–7:00 a.m.	Check email, respond to urgent issues, personal writing
7:00–8:00 a.m.	Family time, commute to the office
8:15–11:45 a.m.	Meetings, working time
11:45 a.m.–1:00 p.m.	Lunch/break time
1:15–3:00 p.m.	Focused working time
3:00–5:00 p.m.	Check email for wrap-up
5:00–6:30 p.m.	Commute, dinner
6:30–10:00 p.m.	Family time, shower
10:00 p.m.–5:00 a.m.	Sleep

Complete your daily schedule:

5:00–6:00 a.m.

6:00–7:00 a.m.

7:00–8:00 a.m.

8:00–9:00 a.m.

9:00–10:00 a.m.

10:00–11:00 a.m.

11:00 a.m.–12:00 p.m.

12:00–1:00 p.m.

1:00–2:00 p.m.

2:00–3:00 p.m.

3:00–4:00 p.m.

4:00–5:00 p.m.

5:00–6:00 p.m.

6:00–7:00 p.m.

7:00–8:00 p.m.

8:00–9:00 p.m.

9:00–10:00 p.m.

10:00–11:00 p.m.

11:00 p.m.–12:00 a.m.

Actions I will take:
1.
2.
3.

RESOURCES

You can do it all, but not by yourself.

In the TRIBE system, time comes first because it's the one thing you can never have again. But what you do with your time depends on your resources. If you want to control your schedule, this is where resources—the R in TRIBE—come into play.

You can't be a leader alone. If you need to accomplish a task, you're not going to do it without help. Every one of us has resources we turn to when we need to get things done, whether we realize it or not. Those resources can be information, objects, services—even people. And knowing what resources are available and when to use them can be the key to advancing your career.

In my work, that sense of understanding what resources were available to me came from frequent communication with my colleagues. I have always been the connector, a point of contact, on teams. Even when I am not the manager, I stay connected with my team with regular one-on-one meetings to make sure I'm supporting everyone's voice. These meetings—even if they're informal coffee chats—help me to hear problems early, listen for trends, and manage team issues with open communication. They also help me to recognize the resources and expertise each team member, including myself, brings to the table, and how they can be utilized to maximize performance.

Diversity is a strength, an integral part of creating balance on a team and giving members a competitive advantage. Each person's individual strengths and experiences need to work together in harmony to create innovative solutions to problems. One person does not have to be everything all the time, but as a team, we should be able to complement each other. Our strengths should supplement the shortcomings of others, and vice versa. Even if reaching out to others isn't natural to you, you should try to communicate with one of your team members every day so you'll be there to help them overcome an obstacle, or give advice on a problem they're currently dealing with, and vice versa.

Just as we need to know how we spend our time in order to change dysfunctional patterns, we need to have an awareness of our resources before we can use them effectively. When I talked with Kelly about how we could get her a better position at work, we analyzed the resources available to her, starting with herself.

We evaluated the skills and talents she brought to the team and the reasons they were important; we analyzed her past performance reviews, circling the words her supervisors repeatedly used and identifying trends. Kelly started to see her strengths: she was strong at coordination, execution, and strategy. But at the same time, she also saw the gaps in her work: she was weak at managing relationships, following through with customers, and updating her team members on her progress.

As Kelly evaluated her resources, she realized that there were many new and advanced skills she had picked up throughout her years on the job. She was better at planning and executing projects than she had realized. She had become more accountable and kept better track of her time. She helped her team members do the same. As her list of skills grew, so did her resentment. By the time we finished the exercise, her face was red with anger. She wondered: If I can do the job and do it well, why isn't my company paying me more to do it?

The truth of the matter was that Kelly did not have a clear career path in mind and was constantly bogged down with the work of others.

In one of our sessions, I asked her if she was ever assigned "extra work." After taking a minute to think about it, Kelly realized that her friends in other departments would often drop off their work at her desk or take her out to lunch to "pick her brain," which caused her to do a lot of extra work without compensation. They used her expertise and her time toward their own projects while she slowly drowned under an ever-increasing workload. This begged the question: Why should Kelly keep doing what she was doing?

Kelly realized that she felt burnt out, depressed, and eternally behind because her coworkers and employer abused her as a resource. It's a common problem when there's a lack of one type of person in a community—that person has to take on more than their fair share because they're being overused.

It was time for Kelly to focus on using resources to *her* benefit. She called in favors from all the people she'd helped; evaluated the tools in her workplace and how she could use them in her hunt for a new job; and applied her experiences to her job search in unique ways. She ensured that every relationship was two-sided, with each party exchanging help and information for something in return. That's the definition of a healthy, "resourceful" relationship.

A Note on Resource Abuse

Resources are there to be used—*productively*. Don't abuse your employers' trust by taking the tools they give you and wasting them. Otherwise, you'll end up like Brad.

When I took over as Brad's team leader, I quickly discovered he was good at telling a story. Between his expensive suits and his use of impressive (if nonsensical) phrases, by the end of our first meeting he'd almost convinced me he had the potential to be a high performer and lead the department. As we were wrapping up, however, I asked, "So what have you been doing since your last assignment?" It was an innocent question—one I asked every member of my team.

Brad stopped in his tracks and smiled broadly. "I found the end of the Internet!"

He enthusiastically told me how he had spent months searching the web for rabbit holes, clicking link to link until he reached a dead end. Then he would start again the next day after sharing what he'd learned that day on his personal blog. Some nights he would stay at the office until midnight searching for the end of an Internet topic. "So is it research for work?" I asked, throwing him a lifeline to connect his browsing behavior with his actual job responsibilities.

"Not really! This company values busyness. My blog keeps me busy!"

The dedication that Brad put into his use of company resources is impressive. Staying in the office late just to ensure he'd completed his task? That took focus and perseverance. Unfortunately, they were misdirected toward an entirely useless, selfish end. By using the tools he'd been given, he was abusing the people who hired him, his coworkers who were forced to do his work for him, and the company's clients who paid for his time.

> "One who causes others misfortunes
> also teaches them wisdom."
> —*African proverb*

Your Resource Toolkit

Now let's apply this resourceful thinking to you and your career. Think about the resources around you: what tools are available to you in your relationships, workplace, and organizations? Go beyond the immediate, obvious answers—anything and anyone can be considered a resource if they teach you something new or assist you in a task.

In order to best use those resources, you have to know what you want to use them *for*—that means prioritizing. Refer to your vision from the first chapter and your journals on time from the previous chapter.

Once you've formed a clear picture of those goals in your mind, it's time to start thinking on how to best accomplish them with the tools at your disposal. Let's start by breaking down the different resources into categories.

> "Hold a true friend with both hands."
> —*African proverb*

Relationship Resources

This category is incredibly broad; the love and comfort your family provides you can be a resource; the college professor who gave you one-on-one sessions could be a resource. But for the purposes of this book, the *primary* relationship resource that will affect your work is the relationships you have with your colleagues. Coworkers help each other out when you need some extra slack, they can share information on clients and practices, and they can be present to offer emotional support.

Identify some of the coworkers whom you trust and what they could best help you with.

As you develop a strong partnership with your coworkers, it can become easy to ignore other parts of the job that deplete your resources. Friendships with coworkers are valuable, but they should not be your most important consideration when it comes time to change jobs.

Changing jobs takes energy and resources, and it oftentimes feels much easier to stay in a position you don't love because you like the people you work with and hope for the job itself to change. If you're having doubts about your career, decide whether you want to find balance in your current job or to find something different. When work seems safe and comfortable, but something else seems to be missing, ask yourself:

- How do I benefit from working with my team? What am I learning?
- Who is here and willing to help me?
- How is this role preparing me for my next opportunity?
- Am I holding onto this job simply because I've invested too much in my coworkers and would feel sad if I left them, even if doing so would make me grow?
- What if, at the end of my life, I begged God for a do-over? Would this job be part of it?

Answering hard questions sometimes leads to necessary realizations.

"However long the night, the dawn will break."
—*African proverb*

Emotional Resources

This category of resources relates back most closely to Time. When you're feeling stressed, do you have resources that will help you to feel at peace? When your workload crushes you, do you have an outlet to divert some of the pressure? Of course, relationships can be an incredibly valuable emotional resource, but they're far from the only one. A hobby that helps you de-stress is an emotional resource, and so is something as simple as lying on your couch, coloring, or taking a well-deserved nap.

Imagine what it would feel like to be emotionally well-resourced. Find the gaps between the way you spend your time and what feeds you (literally and figuratively). Give priority to investing your time on things that build your emotional resources rather than depleting them—whether it's spending time with your family, reading a book, dancing, or getting some extra sleep.

Making time for yourself will break up hectic work schedules and refresh your mind. If you've run low on emotional energy, you will start to feel it everywhere, and it might eventually lead to a breakdown or burnout. Emotional resources are the foundation upon which all other resources rest.

"Wealth if you use it comes to an end;
learning if you use it, increases."
—*Swahili proverb*

Intellectual Resources

Intellectual resources are the things you know from your educational and life experiences. But they also consist of what you *don't* know—things you are interested in learning to either enrich your life, perform better at your job, or both. So, when you think about intellectual resources, don't limit them to what's currently in your brain—include all the things you can draw on to inject *new* knowledge into your mind, whether that's through books, the Internet, intelligent friends, or some other avenue.

Self-reflection is a huge part of gathering intellectual resources. Evaluate your thinking process and search for new insights. Identify the resources you have and the things you are missing. Think about what resources you would like to have and go search for them. I share career and workplace insights to help you professionally grow on the Getting Unstuck with Meredith Moore podcast.

"Bad friends will keep you from having good friends."
—*Gabon proverb*

You Always Have More Resources Than You Think

When I interviewed my father, attorney and entrepreneur Mr. Cornell Leverette Moore, for this project, he marveled at the number of resources available for my generation to rely on. He grew up in the Jim Crow–era South, which meant that at the beginning of his career, he didn't have a template—or access to mentors and role models beyond his family. However, my father doesn't view his situation as one of complete disadvantage—in many ways, he's grateful that he had to forge his own path in life. A lack of resources meant he was free to be creative, to make his own rules, and to come up with solutions that were innovative precisely because he'd had to carefully think them through.

He compared his situation to mine by likening his resource library to a blank sheet of paper, versus a sheet that had been filled out with instructions. And he's right—my generation has tutorials, tips, and instructions *everywhere*—instant digital resources available through the public library system, YouTube, Google, you name it.

A Google search is an *amazing* resource, even though it may seem so commonplace that you don't even think of it as such. You have a wealth of information at your fingertips—instructions from experts in your field, personal testimony from people who have found themselves in a situation similar to yours, and anything else you might desire.

So if you ever feel stuck, just remember that you always have the world's biggest resource right there on your phone. Use it to give yourself a little nudge.

Taking Charge

Once you've identified your resources, it's time to start using them to their fullest potential. Get fierce and focused on taking charge of your life.

Sit down with your coworkers, friends, and other people you regularly interact with—specifically the ones you've helped without getting much in return. Let them know that you will no longer take on extra work if it comes at the expense of your well-being. If these people genuinely *do* care about you, they'll work to rectify their error and help you turn a one-way drain on your time and emotional resources into a productive, reciprocal relationship. If they *don't* truly care and continue in old habits, cut off the relationship or encourage them to be more self-reliant.

Reassess your schedule from the Time chapter. Make sure your schedule allows for emotional resources that will keep you calm, productive, and relaxed. The more stress you're under, the less and less useful you'll be in any aspect of your life.

Set aside a certain period per day or week to build your intellectual resources. Research strategies to improve your company, read books and articles on how to improve your performance, or even engage with material that enriches your knowledge of a non-work-related personal interest. Attend speaking events or set up informational interviews. You are worth your time!

If you feel your work is underappreciated, talk to your bosses and explain your true value. Sometimes your bosses are just unaware of all you do, especially if you take on extra work for your coworkers. Consider requesting extra resources in return for your time—after all, money is one of the most useful resources of all.

ACTIVITY 3: RESOURCE MAP

Any time you find yourself overtaxed and aren't sure how to recover, do this activity and ask yourself if you've forgotten some of the resources that can prove invaluable to your current situation.

Answer the following questions in your journal:

Relationships

List all the people in your day-to-day life.

- What functions do my relationships fulfill?
- What kind of unique capabilities do these people have?
- Which of my friends and colleagues can I call on when I need help?
- How can I raise the bar and embrace a higher standard?

Education

List all of the subjects you're knowledgeable about and what skills you have.

- Which aspects of my education have I retained the most knowledge of?
- Has there ever been a time when something I learned became unexpectedly useful?
- How well did my education prepare me for my current position?

- What have I learned outside of the educational experience that enriched and improved me?
- What are places I can go when I need answers to questions I'm unsure of?

Workplace

- What opportunities and resources does my workplace provide me as an employee? Am I taking advantage of everything that's provided for me?
- Are there certain resources I could introduce to the workplace that would make everyone's job easier? How could I bring these ideas to the decision makers?
- Am I considered a useful resource by leadership? What do people thank me for?
- Who can/will help me in difficult times?
- Who has left me in difficult times?
- Who PUT me in difficult times? (WATCH OUT!)

Personal Life

- What are some aspects of my non-work life that I can use as a resource in the workplace?
- What are the boundaries I've set up between my personal life and my work life?
- Who can/will help me in my next transition?
- Who has experienced the challenges I'm facing?

- What am I most anxious about? What am I losing sleep over?

Actions I will take:

1.
2.
3.

> "You learn how to cut down trees
> by cutting them down."
> —*Bateke proverb*

INNOVATION

You have the power to see your life differently.

When I graduated Howard University in 2004, I was selected for Lincoln Financial Group's coveted Professional Development Program. The goal of the program was to attract top talent with diverse perspectives, assimilate these candidates into complex financial institutions, and find better integration strategies for talent management. The benefit of being in this program was that I was exposed to a network of high-potential, talented people from different backgrounds and sectors. This exposure helped me consider different paths for my career. By building a rapport and trust with a wide range of professionals, I became comfortable asking for advice, perspectives, and feedback.

Although I look back on my years in training as some of the best in my career, they also taught me too early to depend on a corporation's resources to handle my professional development. I relied too much on the processes of an engaged senior management team to prepare me for my next assignment. Gradually, I became lost in the executive shuffle of working in elite corporate America. Grit and getting things done became less important than my memorization of key personnel or my ability to get my manager's lunch order on time. In trying to focus on being the best at the tasks included in my role, I became myopic, and failed to think outside the box.

I believed that by doing my current job to the best of my ability, without deviation, I was preparing for success with the company long-term.

At one point, I considered staying at one job because the challenges and lack of support at work made me doubt I had the energy to start my own business or learn a new corporate culture. If things were this bad where I was, who knew what they would be like starting all over? I had spent so long memorizing the corporate minutiae at my current position—who knew how long it would take me to do that all over again? I felt scared that something bad would happen—that I would fail, or that my coworkers would retaliate against me for taking time to focus on myself.

Relying on resources that had been handed to me had stunted my creativity and my ability to grow. They'd shrunk what made me, *me*.

I started to feel guilty for wanting to be valued at work,

becoming overly critical of myself and comparing my work to that of others'. I was starting to get depressed and lose faith in my ability to change my work situation.

Kelly felt it too. We started to doubt if we could make a difference. It felt like it was too late, and our goals were unrealistic. Four months into our mentoring sessions, we stopped going to lunch. Six months in, we avoided talking about anything outside of work. We were under deadlines, and during budget season we were too tired once the day was done to stay and talk any longer after work. I started to appreciate having an absent manager with low expectations when my kids got sick or when I needed a few extra hours during the holidays.

Nobody noticed or cared when Kelly and I stopped coming in early to work, or putting in our best effort when we were there. We were once again becoming parts of a greater machine.

Gut check: How much do I like what I do each day?

Reviewing my journal helped me to see I did not want to change my goals—I wanted a workplace that would support my mental health and my vision for my life. I wrote, *"Fear, stress, and anger narrow the mind. I want a workplace where I am not afraid of how people will react to me being different.*

Life is about what you do with your time. How can I push Kelly forward, and watch her as I remain behind? How can I send someone else out of the window and not be willing to jump? I feel sick thinking about how long I can do this. Is it a good thing to merely survive? Don't I deserve to thrive? I feel like everyone thinks my happiness is a joke and I should be happy to have a check. I guess I thought I was working toward a different goal, but now I don't know who's right. I don't want to go to work. I wish tomorrow were a snow day and work were canceled."

Reading this entry over was the moment when everything changed. I decided I would finally take real action, to participate in my *own* rescue. This is the number-one way to create lasting change. I finally was ready to put my happiness, personal fulfillment, and respect for myself first. This was something only *I* could do, and no one else.

It was time to stop going only by the corporate playbook.

The Limits of Resources

Looking back at the whole beginning of this chapter, you might think something isn't clicking here. *You have a whole chapter on resources! They're already part of this book! How could you possibly be depending too much on your corporation's resources?*

It's true, using the resources available to you is important.

It's why they're there, and deliberately depriving yourself of them will only result in an inability to perform your job to the best of your ability. That said—if *all* you're doing is relying on company resources to get your job done, it's bad for the company and it's bad for you. The only growth you will experience will be handed to you; rather than becoming your own person, you'll be copying and pasting aspects of yourself from a company template. And when you're just the same as everyone else, there's no real reason for the company to keep you around. *Anyone* could do your job provided they used the same resources.

No, employers should not want to keep you around simply because you can follow instructions to the letter. The reason your employers should keep you around—the reason you should be hired in the first place—is that you bring things to the job that are unique to you. Resources are all well and good, but they can only be used for a limited set of circumstances, and following their instructions to the letter will *never* result in creative ways of problem-solving.

That doesn't mean that you have to create systems and solutions out of thin air. Innovation, the I in TRIBE, isn't about making something new. It simply means that you think of something differently.

Innovation is about seeing your life as malleable and imagining yourself as someone who is able to direct change.

Innovation is about discovering how disconnected things connect and then affect the future.

Innovation is about seeing how the true nature of a problem could be entirely different from the way it's been perceived up until now. It starts with considering other ideas, being creative, and expanding your mind while suspending your reality. Letting your mind consider what's possible makes you more creative.

Innovation as a Lifestyle

As I started in corporate America, a place where I assumed everyone would strive to be the same, I initially found some of my colleagues' creativity to be a bit of a shock. They ate, slept, and drank creatively. In the office, I saw everything from hammer pants and platform shoes made of doll parts to people making stews on desktop warmers. Talented people are expected to be nontraditional—it's part of the appeal—and it's widely accepted that high performers are allowed to be exotic and make demands to create their ideal work environment.

The longer I paid attention, the more I was inspired by people who brought their whole selves to work. It began to sink in for me that innovation was a lifestyle, not simply a product. The idea that within our workplace we were as safe as we were in our homes, or even *more* safe to take risks, changed my opinion of work.

Innovation and personal expression all has to do with an ethic of self-care. When I cut my hair off, wear colorful floral jumpsuits, show people my tattoos, or change my appearance in any other way that makes me more comfortable, I am doing so with integrity and authenticity because it's in my best interest and who I am, and it makes me feel freer to be more productive and creative at work.

If there are little things you can do for yourself that put you in a better state of mind for your job, why not do them? This ethic extends beyond appearance. I never book flights back-to-back, and I try to schedule a mandatory day off before and after I travel to help myself recuperate. When I take care of myself, it helps me stay present for others and bring my all to the office.

Of course, you can't take this too far—if everyone is able to do whatever they want in the workplace in the name of "freedom," it's anarchy, not a corporation. And it *is* possible to delude yourself into thinking that doing whatever you want is an expression of creativity when you're not really finding innovative ways to do much of anything. You can't simply wear personality quirks as a surface decoration— you have to apply your mind-set to things beyond personal appearance and behavior. It's at that point that the quirks you display are accepted as an extension of your innovation, not simply attention-hungry gimmicks.

For example, when I first decided to have my tattoos visible in the workplace, it was not simply a cavalier decision. I was running a risk—the classic image of a corporate American executive does not include inked skin. My choice to do this was an extension of my desire not to let my job stifle my personal identity and aspirations.

My freedom tattoo is a symbol to other coworkers that they shouldn't be afraid to let important parts of their lives into their career. As a black woman, I already was visibly outside the norm. By showing my body art, I was making a deeper statement about the value of diversity in a homogenous workplace. If I had just flippantly decided to show my tattoos, it wouldn't have meant anything; because I had reasons for my decision, it became an example of purposeful innovation.

Considering Your Background

So much of who we are—our temperament, our opinions, our values—comes from the environment we were raised in. How we grew up is a major factor in determining our personhood, more than almost anything else. The same applies, to a lesser extent, to adulthood—the circumstances in which we find ourselves will shape and mold our personality.

When you're looking for ways you can innovate, consider how your life situation has equipped you to deal with things from a perspective that others don't necessarily have. For instance, when my dad was ascending in his career, he noted that being a Black man in America has obvious social disadvantages. He understands what it was like to live in a world that would try to grind him down. He used to tell me, "The world knows who you are, so if you don't know who you are, you are in trouble." It also meant that, as he got closer to the top, he knew better than to rub it in people's faces and become obnoxiously joyous in his success—he'd lived with a lack of privilege long enough to know that gloating about his position was not going to do him any favors.

So, even though growing up as a Black man in America presented him with difficulties, he was able to take his background and glean those lessons from it for the future, lessons that white people in his field could not have learned in the same way, and it made him consider his decisions differently as a result.

You may not come from the same background as me, or my father, or any number of other people who have been successful in their workplace, but you *do* have a unique life story, one that no one else can replicate. So ask yourself: what about your past and present living situation has taught you to think in ways that others might not? Are there certain aspects of your background that have disadvantaged you, but also taught you lessons? How can you apply those lessons to innovation?

Measuring Innovation

One of the best ways to figure out how you can innovate at work is to look at other areas of life and try to spot unique approaches you've taken to the problems you've encountered there. No matter the context—a family argument, broken plumbing, trying to balance an impossible schedule—was there ever a problem that seemed insurmountable to you and/or others until you considered it from a fresh angle?

Now, ask yourself—how can you bring that angle of thinking to problems in your workplace? Obviously, there won't always be a direct correlation between the problems you encounter at work and the problems you encounter with your bathroom plumbing, but you should still be able to take a set of behaviors and viewpoints that are successful in one area of your life and apply them to another.

A few years into his career with McDonald's, my mentor Don Thompson moved into operations working at a

Chicago location of the restaurant, starting from the ground up. Today it might seem crazy, but he wanted to truly understand this gigantic company he was trying to run. He moved from fry cook to manager quickly, and by the end of his rotation, he'd learned a lot. When he went back to pursuing his executive track, he took his work on the front counter with him.

Later, when Don's speeches had to explain the importance of migration paths and growth strategies, he emphasized to me that we needed to recognize managers, especially those who led in sales and customer service. They had strategies that we could take from a single restaurant and apply it on a company-wide level.

The strategy worked, but it only could have happened with a diverse team led by someone unique like Mr. Thompson, an executive who had put in the work on the ground and understood its importance.

You are (or have the potential to be) a change-maker, an idea person, someone whose unique approaches to problems are emulated and remembered. Your legacy will be cemented not by what you do but *how* you do it—whether you did things the way everyone else did or stood out.

Do What You Can Do

A word of caution: focusing on doing the things only you can do does not mean turning yourself into a superhero.

As I've traveled the world, I've realized more and more that, in the grand scheme of things, I'm ultimately powerless and small. As a younger executive, I'd fallen victim to the idea that I had the power to totally rewrite the rules and change things all by myself. And while you might *think* that's the case, your work should be about more than that. It should be about lifting up those around you, being compassionate, and setting an example so that *everyone* at the company benefits. Innovation doesn't equal single-handedly saving things; it means evaluating yourself, understanding the unique things you do best, and using them to the benefit of everyone.

During my life, I've reinvented myself many times. I thought of myself as a journalist when I was in college. When I worked in finance, that also became part of my identity. My self-image changed when I interned at a PR agency, and when I became a vegan. I began to explore new passions as a speechwriter at McDonald's, and again at 3M as a scientist. When I worked at Comcast, I grew comfortable with the idea of being in media and technology.

With each revision, you add another unique element to the overall person that is you. It's an empowering feeling to realize that you've added multiple different skill sets to your toolbox, further increasing your ability to solve problems with a unique approach. When you reinvent yourself, or even aspects of yourself, it can motivate you to change the world around you as well. However, it's important not to become discouraged when we feel helpless, and to realize that any small way we can contribute to the betterment of the world is a victory, rather than banking on large-scale changes once we take the steps to innovate.

> "Ears that do not listen to advice
> accompany the head when it's cut off."
> —*African proverb*

Two years after Hurricane Katrina, I visited schools and homes in New Orleans to help assess how the distribution channels McDonald's uses to run their business can be used for disaster preparedness. I'd expected the city to be fairly back to normal so long after the disaster had hit, but the sights that greeted us staggered me.

The problems in philanthropy are complex and big: racism, poverty, disaster recovery, human trafficking, hunger, homelessness, violence against women and children—the list goes on and on. Our guide showed us a block where every single inhabitant had died; even after all this time, the damage was overwhelming. In many places, there hadn't even been attempts to rebuild. I met a little girl who had been left with no family after the hurricane. She became very attached to me, and I desperately wanted to help her. I couldn't adopt a daughter or move to New Orleans, but my emotions consumed me and I felt alone and powerless.

In New Orleans, with this girl in my arms, I faced the painful reality and frustration because I knew I needed to do more. But I had no idea how one person could impact a problem so massive.

I called my mother, who is a leader in philanthropy. As the first African American woman chair of the W.K. Kellogg Foundation, she traveled globally, addressing these issues and the systems that create them. My mom immediately recognized my emotional overload. She knew I felt overwhelmed and could hear the empathy in my voice. I pleaded with her to tell me what to do. I had the resources of a corporation, but I felt powerless.

She asked me, "Meredith, why are you there? Why do you think they sent YOU?" I sat quietly, nothing came to mind.

"Because it's my job," I answered.

"Yes, and they know you care. They know you'll do something, they know you won't stop until you do your best. Do that. Start there. Build a team." She wanted me to prioritize *how* I could help.

Sometimes we need to work with the systems that are in place to help and realize that we can't take on the burdens of the world. So I did what I could with the resources that I had. People needed power and fresh water, neither of which were readily available. I knew that McDonald's had generators, water, ice, and a ready-made supply chain that was able to restore services quickly with the help of partners like Coca Cola and Wal-Mart. Most of the companies that contributed to the relief efforts had no plan or structure in place for disaster aid, yet we all had employees whose lives were forever altered. We knew we had to do something for the community. I worked on a tight timeline to establish a McDonald's foundation and created a disaster relief plan so we could bring help faster next time.

I don't know what happened to the little girl, but I know that I did my best to deliver company resources to those in need. Even though the complete scale of devastation was demoralizing, we figured out a way where we could make an impact, however small. Take joy in helping others, even when you know that you can't fix the world. I always want to do more, but sometimes innovation doesn't mean a radical shift—it can be as simple as making sure someone gets clean water for the week.

Working without Innovation

When I worked in PR, I was always looking for brand ambassadors, and Theodore fit the bill. He was assigned to my project team because he had worked for my company for a long time. He had led programs that were approved by executives and never received negative feedback. He was attractive, well-spoken, and had the company jargon down pat. He also looked the part of a high performer, coming into the interview with me on a Tuesday dressed in a three-piece suit and dress shoes. Before Theodore could take a seat, he was telling me all of the things he worked on and why he was important to "higher-ups above my paygrade." He explained away a recent demotion as evidence of the "critical realignment of his responsibilities to reflect the company's focus on maximizing performance and diversity."

He talked a good game, but I was personally disappointed watching the onstage/backstage performance of Theodore. Behind all that talk was . . . nothing, really. If he had a unique perspective on issues at work, he didn't voice it. If he had creative ways to solve problems, they were never brought up. None of this was what I needed in a brand ambassador.

I soon realized that his coworkers had lost faith in the company's performance metrics and doubted that anyone really cared if they did their work. If Theodore's all-style-no-substance performance made him successful, what was the point of actually working? Word was spreading that making small talk and looking busy were enough.

When his performance review rolled around, I lowered Theodore's performance rating. As a new leader in the organization, I didn't want my collaborative management style, which is already laid-back and empowering, to be abused or associated with Theodore's pseudo-work.

During a subsequent talent meeting, a colleague asked me why I'd done so, questioning why I didn't think Theodore was a leader or ready for more responsibility. This colleague said he felt Theodore should be marked to be my replacement—he felt strongly that Theodore could do my job and wanted to know the timeline for his promotion. I was confused and shocked. Normally department performance plans are not debated unless someone wants to poach talent from another area.

"You seem to see a lot of potential in Theodore—would you like him to join your team?"

The manager's face turned red. "No . . . my team is full. I was just asking. Don't get defensive."

I calmed myself by taking a long sip of water. Being called defensive communicated in that moment that that colleague thought I was being emotional, overly passionate, and unreasonable in my decision, a common attack on women in leadership roles.

The person questioning my assessment of Theodore was his friend. We weren't discussing logic, he was defending his buddy.

If you work without truly innovating, you may be able to move forward to a certain extent. But once you hit a certain point, it will be obvious to everyone that you're not serving a purpose. When Theodore no longer had his friends as a shield, his role was terminated. Had he truly cared about adding value to his work and had brought a unique perspective rather than some fancy jargon, it wouldn't have happened.

Breaking Free

Givers must create boundaries because takers never will. In a way, Kelly and I were right to be depressed about our ability to change things in the workplace. Functioning as we were, we were simply cogs in the machine—doing our best to fulfill the pile of corporate duties dumped on top of us rather than approaching things through a shifting paradigm.

Kelly started looking at the ways in which she was innovative—considering the little things that brought her joy at work and skills that were unique to her. When the company hired Kelly, they'd assigned her to a team that was big on social interaction. Everyone else wanted to solve problems through social influence and office politics. Kelly, meanwhile, was all about the details. Meeting deadlines, taking notes, keeping track of data—these were all things she loved to do, things that were embedded in her work style. In a balanced team, these skills are key, but when a company hires too many employees with similar work styles, it can leave a department unbalanced and lets too much of a certain type of work fall on the shoulders of one person.

In the context of our work environment, Kelly's workflow was totally at odds with everyone else's, and all the detail-oriented stuff she was good at ended up falling squarely on her shoulders. If she didn't do it, no one would. That's a recipe for isolation and exhaustion, so it's no wonder she got sick of where she was. *But*, her unique point of view also meant that she was already a master innovator. She had to be—she was the sole type A employee on her team who could pick up everyone else's slack, which meant she had to come up with constant solutions, and fast. While this was a terrible position for her to be in, it also meant that when her next job came along, she'd have more than her fair share of unique solutions, viewpoints, and ideas to bring to the table. And her continued devotion to her unique workstyle in spite of the challenges it caused proved that it was a part of who she was. She was dedicated to doing things from her own point of view, and that's what innovation is all about: being different.

Kelly left the company a few weeks after I did. She went through an arbitration process to hold the company accountable for how they kept her in a stagnant position for years, underpaid her, and alienated her as a mother. Though I had my own bones to pick with the company, I ultimately decided that the arbitration process was not worth the effort. I understood the power dynamics of the corporate structure and wasn't optimistic that I would get results as a black woman.

Kelly, however, was in a privileged position to effect change, and she took the opportunity. She wanted documentation of her case to help the company learn from their oversights, and do some innovation of their own. During the arbitration, she also searched for other jobs.

Kelly had always identified as a worker bee, but that was before she outgrew her position. She began to envision a new identity that was more closely associated with senior personnel. During meetings, she would write notes to herself about the things she would do again and the things she would avoid in the future. The lists grew as we brainstormed descriptions of her ideal job. She listed all the things that the company relied on her to do but that weren't in her official job description.

Through these self-exploration exercises, she came up with a list of questions to ask potential employers about their work cultures:

1. How do you describe the ideal employee here? What time do people arrive at work? What time do they leave for the day?
2. What are some general words you would use to describe the work environment?
3. How do you develop relationships with managers and leaders? How do you gain visibility to be selected for leadership development and awards? What do you tell your mentors about your impact at work?
4. How much input do you have on the strategic direction of the organization?
5. Do you have friendships at work that you feel are meaningful to your personal development?
6. Do you feel safe and supported at work?
7. How do employees submit feedback? How often do they utilize these options? How does the company handle their feedback, even when it's critical?
8. How does the team handle conflict and crisis?

9. What does it take to get promoted? Are you seen as a leader or an executive here?

Then, Kelly tried a technique that I use when I'm looking for a new position. She thoughtfully selected three companies to apply to, based on how their work cultures aligned with her own values. In her application, she explained why she thought she would be a good fit for the company, and why the company would be a good fit for her. Her explanations showed them that she was someone who was sensitive to existing culture and sincerely wanted her next job to be a good fit.

Feeling stuck in your career? When your search efforts for a new position start to stall, work with a career coach to review your plan and keep you on track and accountable.

Before long, Kelly had a new position in a global headquarters, three levels away from the CEO. At the company we worked at together, she was thirty-six levels away.

Even more exciting, in her new job, Kelly managed a budget and helped plan events as part of her job description rather than having these responsibilities lobbed to her as additional work.

While her old company eventually fired the employees

who held her back, she recognized that the same work culture was still in place once those people left. In her new job, she was able to take a leadership role to help create a better work culture. She started programs that supported women, including a mentorship program. Thanks to her soul-searching, Kelly was able to invent a new identity and position for herself that not only made her happier and emphasized all the skills her last company took for granted, but also let her make lasting change for others.

Kelly's story is just one example of a principle I learned over and over in my career: companies don't just pay their employees with money, but also with experience. If the experience of your current job doesn't help you develop professionally, then you might have to leave in order to get ahead.

Once you figure out what experiences will help you to gain unique, innovative perspectives and ideas, chase after them. You deserve to be passionate about your work, and your work should help you live with integrity—to be personable, friendly, real, and honest.

ACTIVITY 4: INNOVATE YOUR LIFE VISION BOARD

I create a vision board each year to keep my goals and guiding statements from this book's initial chapter in front of me. Seeing your goals on a daily basis increases your chances of making progress because you are more aware of what you want and how you need to get there. I keep one master vision board in my office and a more personal, focused board in my bathroom.

Start by taking a big piece of paper and divide your life into the six areas below. Find ways to innovate in each area and write them down. When you're finished, look through magazines for pictures that will remind you of what you want. Post the board somewhere you'll see it every day.

Relationships

- What relationships are important to me?
- Who do I need to nurture?
- Who do I need to release?
- Who can help me stay on track? Who inspires me to do better?

Find pictures of how you want relationships to make you feel and activities you would like to share.

Career

- How am I monetizing my talent?
- What's next in my career? What milestones would motivate me to do my best?
- Who do I admire? How can I imitate their positive attributes?
- What does balance or harmony mean to me?
- What can only I do? How can I enact my gifts in my life?

Think of interesting milestones in your career and personal life like graduations, travel, and community service.

Physical

- What do I physically need to achieve my goals?
- How am I caring for my physical well-being?
- Am I doing everything I can for my health? Are there any areas of my life where I need to take action (i.e. regular exercise, diet, self-care)?

Look for pictures of fitness, activities you'd like to try, medicines you'd like to stop taking.

Spiritual

- Who am I called to serve?

- What problem am I solving?
- What am I divinely called to do?
- What makes me special? What do I have to offer the spiritual power I serve?
- What do I see as my spiritual legacy?

Look for pictures of significance that show your passion and reinforce your beliefs.

Financial

- What financial decisions am I preparing for?
- If I believed in my dream, what would I do in six months? Twelve months?
- How will I invest in my vision?
- What is my happiness worth? What resources do I have?

Find pictures that represent what you want to be true about your finances, what you want to be able to support or things you want to invest in.

Education/Growth

- Where will my dreams take me?
- Who will help me bring my vision to life?
- Who can support me when it's challenging?
- What do I want to attract?

- What do I want to learn to help me do the things only I can do?

Search for pictures of inspirational quotes and topics that interest you.

As you map out these areas of your life, seek connections and overarching themes. Look over what you have done, and ask yourself, what can only you do? What barriers or challenges do you see for the next twelve to eighteen months? How can you innovate past them?

Affirmations
- I am doing the work to live the life of my dreams.
- I am proud of myself and all I've accomplished.
- I am becoming the woman I was meant to be.
- I surrender my power to the creator of the universe and ask you to do your will and work your magic in your own divine timing to deliver what is only for me.

Actions I will take:
1.
2.
3.

BELIEF

Everything you think is already in existence.

Each company has a tagline. From "Just Do It" to "I'm Lovin' It," great brands sum themselves up in a few words. These slogans are about more than catching potential customers' interests. They're miniature values statements, representatives of what each company strives to present to you through its product or service. And those statements should indicate to you that, even at the advertising level, values, ideologies, and beliefs are important. In this chapter, we will discuss strategies to incorporate your own beliefs, values, and faith into your work.

First, let me define the word "belief" in the context of this chapter and the rest of the book. My personal beliefs center in the perfect universe, in trusting the Creator and flow of her Creation. It's about my willingness to trust what's intrinsic to me to guide my thoughts and direct me.

Your own beliefs might be quite different.

Do you trust yourself to guide your life, or have you ever

talked back to your inner voice? Do you have faith in a personal deity, or something broader? Do you primarily define yourself by your spiritual beliefs or a more personal set of values?

From that belief, extrapolate what your core values are. Mine include:

- education
- community
- freedom
- spirituality
- curiosity
- love

Regardless of what your beliefs are, a toxic workplace can erase your ability to hold them with positive energy. Too much of American work culture thinks of the workplace as a dungeon of some kind, a punishing experience that rewards you when you keep your head down. To many, the only way to get through it is to lace your conversations with a healthy dose of sarcasm and cynicism. And trust me, I absolutely get that. Work can suck. And cynicism can feel great in the moment—it's an instant coping mechanism and also serves to make you look "above it all."

But the more you use cynicism as a defense mechanism, the more you'll simply end up feeling drained and empty in the long term. You won't feel good about your work, and when you're remembered by the people who worked alongside you, they'll think of you as the snarky person, or worse, the one who undermined the team. Sarcasm is not inspiring; it can make others feel small and will reduce your ability to influence others because no one will want to work with you.

That's not to say you need to spend all your time at work being *happy*. Happiness isn't what this is about—belief is not an inherently happy thing. Rather than seeking happiness, you should seek purpose. Rather than acting as though nothing you do matters, you should try to imbue everything you do at your office with meaning.

Every single one of my mentors in my career has had a deep commitment to living their values, no matter the circumstance. They have lived their personal ethics, fought for causes they believed in, and tried to pass their wisdom on to others. I guarantee you that the correlation between this and their personal growth and success is no accident.

They were able to turn their workplaces into the place where they became better people—the rewards they received were not just material, but spiritual. And not only did they improve themselves, they had an impact on everyone around them. I'm a better person for learning from these people, and I know I'm only one of millions inspired by their stories.

You don't have to transform into a happy working robot when you show up for your job. You don't have to pretend that stupid, pointless things can't happen at your office. But when you bring your values to the workplace with you, you will have an experience you never could have gotten from cynicism. With practice, you'll be less bothered by what you can't control.

Believing in the Workplace

When I was early in my career, I worried that my workplace would be hostile to my beliefs. Luckily, that's not always the case. Take Cindy Kent, or as I like to call her, spiritual Superwoman.

While we often tell each other, "God won't give you more than you can bear," there are times in life when things get too overwhelming and scary to go on. In those times, we can find ourselves in denial, suffering, and silence when we need to be asking for help. When I feel those dark moments and start to lose sight of my beliefs, I remember my conversations with Cindy.

In her career, Cindy has found what's most important for her, and she's connected that purpose to all aspects of her daily life, her career, and beyond. Out of everyone I've ever met, she's the one who lives her life the most *on purpose.*

I had the privilege of working with Cindy at 3M and as a member of the Minneapolis–St. Paul chapter of The Links, Incorporated, a civic organization for African American women founded in Philadelphia in 1943. In this work, we were imbued with purpose by our values of caring for others and caring for ourselves. Cindy's passion is healthcare. She taught me the value of self-care because if we're constantly fighting for health care and basic needs, we can't set realistic goals or share our talents. Black women born in 2010 have a life expectancy of 77.2 years (four to six years fewer than any other racial group); one in five have mood disorders, anxiety or phobias, substance abuse issues, antisocial tendencies, and high stress.

High stress is especially of concern for women like Cindy and me. The price of leadership is stress, and understanding your limits is critical to being able to lead your own life. Cindy always lets me be me, and has always been herself in return.

Five years into her career, Cindy decided she wanted to go back to graduate school full-time. Not just for any degree, though—she wanted to get her master's in divinity and her MBA in marketing. It would be easy, in this situation, to imagine company resistance to what might seem like a pretty random degree in corporate America's eyes. So Cindy was floored when her company's chief human resource officer called to let her know that her employers wanted to sponsor her in this venture! He explained to her, "We can go get leaders from any business school in the nation or the world, but what we can't teach is your empathy, the way that you lead, and the way people are inspired and follow you, even at lower levels of the organization. We believe that your divinity training will only refine and enhance those aspects of your work."

On the face of it, Cindy's situation appears exceptional— not every company will help finance a combined divinity and marketing degree for an engineer. And that's true. But if your company has good leaders, in touch with the needs of the workforce and the world, they've probably already realized that you're at your best when you're living your beliefs. The best management teams understand this. They want you to be proud of your work and see it as an extension of your identity, so you will give your highest quality work, defend the brand, and participate in volunteer activities. They *want* you to honor your beliefs and ideals because they know that's what makes you an effective employee and inspiring figure. And in Cindy's case, their investment in her divinity degree reaped huge rewards, not only for her but for them.

After all, employees don't check their emotions at the door when they enter the office—they're often dealing with stress, pain, and other negative experiences, and having a leader who's been equipped to deal with that sort of situation can be hugely beneficial to an organization.

What worked for her worked for me as well—when I was working at McDonald's, Don Thompson told me the company was going to fund 90 percent of my tuition for my master's of science degree in managerial communications at Northwestern University. My master's degree has been invaluable to my career, just like Mr. Thompson recognized it would be. Because it would make me a better employee, the company got behind me.

While your workplace may not decide to fund your attempt to get a master's degree in the humanities, you'll be surprised at the steps they'll take to accommodate an expression of your values. They recognize that it makes a difference, extending in ripples from your own life outward.

Cindy sums up the importance of following beliefs this way: work and life are not two independent spheres. They overlap and intertwine, and any compartmentalization present between them is an illusion on our part. We don't suddenly become a separate person when we leave home and head to work. Who we are remains the same—all of our lived experience travels with us, and that includes our beliefs.

True Change

One of the most important parts of bringing your beliefs to work is recognizing when it's time to let go.

When it finally came time for me to leave the company where I worked with Kelly, it was impossible for me to make a plan to leave without telling my team. Every time I quit a company, someone tells me it's a bad idea to announce your decision, but as a leader I don't believe in surprises.

The first time I told Kelly I was going to quit, she tried to talk me out of it. She said things were finally starting to improve with me in charge and that she could see my leadership style was rubbing off on others. I asked her what she thought would happen if I quit.

"It will all go away," she said quickly. "If you leave, things will go back to what they were before."

"Then the change isn't real," I said. "If I'm the only one doing it genuinely, then it's just me. When everyone believes, then it's authentic, then it's the culture."

Simply following leaders to make them happy may work in the short term, but if you truly want to change your workplace culture for the better, lip service isn't enough. It is absolutely essential that you be genuine in living your beliefs in the workplace. Being a leader means believing you can set enough of an example that your colleagues follow your lead, even after you've gone. And if once you leave, others eventually return to their old ways? You were still true to yourself, regardless of what others thought, and may still have made a difference to someone, somewhere in that company.

Each morning I pray and ask for help to see the whole world as not a bustling mob of strangers, but as my human family. I ask for support, enlightenment, and forgiveness. For me, apologizing is not about weakness when it is authentic. Acknowledging where I could improve is how I hold myself accountable. It's that accountability that is perhaps the greatest benefit of living for your beliefs. No matter what you do, you're always doing it with the knowledge that you are responsible and can always be better.

ACTIVITY 5: THE POWER OF BELIEF

STEP 1:

Who do you believe in?

Make a list of the five people in your life who have done the most to shape who you are. They could be family, friends, teachers, bosses, or even fictional television characters. Evaluate each one with the following questions:

1. What aspects of this person do I admire?
2. In what areas are they imperfect?
3. What lessons has this person taught me?
4. How long has this person been an influence on my life?

Once the questions for each have been answered, compare the five people. What do they share in common? How have they impacted you differently?

STEP 2:

Now, make a list of the three values you hold dearest in your life. Answer the following questions about each:

1. When did this value become important to me?
2. How will living this value bring me more joy?
3. What actions do I feel exemplify this value?

STEP 3:

How do you make others believe?

Finally, look at yourself through the lens of your important values.

1. Do I feel I exhibit these values in my own life?
2. Have other people told me that I inspire them with my personal example? Do they follow similar values?
3. Have I noticed a shift in the actions and beliefs of others around me that could be attributed to me?
4. How can I live every day to encourage people to follow my example and practice the values I find important?

Congratulations! You've now claimed your time, reviewed your resources, invested in your own innovation and committed to living your core beliefs. But if you're anything like me, you might be feeling overwhelmed or anxious. You've done a lot! It might be time to take a break.

Here are my favorite ways to recover when I need time to process the TRIBE steps:

- Have a lunch date with a friend.
- Spend twenty-four hours without social media.
- Get outside and enjoy nature.
- Make it a movie night, give yourself a break, and veg out.

- Think of others. Give your day to serving your community.
- Get wet. Spending time in a pool, on a beach, or in the lake always helps me reset.
- Make time for a date night and check in with your loved ones.
- Attend a retreat with me on a tropical island and build your network of people to support your vision.

Actions I will take:

1.

2.

3.

EVOLUTION

I trust the universe wants to move me forward.

Evolution has been a hugely important theme of my life. However, it's not just change for the sake of change. Evolution is about making your impact clearly apparent to the world. It's about creating lasting change in yourself and in your environment.

Learning to make smart decisions, improving over time, and making tomorrow better—for me and for other people—are what drive me. And in my experience, this desire is one of the few that could be called universal. Every person and every culture is different, but one constant that holds them together is this drive for constant improvement—it crosses races, religions, countries, and any other barrier (real or imagined) that you can think of. It is the primary force behind all change large and small.

Setting Your Course

Each time I made a change in my career, my parents

disagreed with my decision. My family questioned my judgment, something I saw mirrored at work from coworkers as well. But I knew that evolution requires risk-taking and that means being confident you can be someone different—and better—than who you were today.

When I decided to quit my job in PR to work at McDonald's, all my dad said was that the rent is due on the first, and they don't take coupons. He couldn't understand why I would start over again just a few weeks after starting a promising career at a Chicago agency where I was working on big accounts. But I knew I wasn't going to be happy there or make my mark.

One day, during the time I was still working there, I was standing in the pouring rain, waiting on the bus I took to get to work. As the water poured down onto me, I felt stuck, wet, and miserable in a job that felt like it was getting me nowhere fast. I started thinking about what I wanted and made a list in my head:

- A job that would allow me to drive into underground parking and avoid the weather.
- A manager who would care more about my work getting done than whether I was at my desk at 8:00 a.m.
- A salary that would pay for a car and parking.

I made my list, item after item running through my

head, and by the time I arrived at my office, I knew I had to quit.

My job didn't check any items off the list. I had started at the firm as a twenty-five-year-old intern, and had already invested so much time and effort into advancing my position, but I realized I would never get to the level in my career that I wanted without making some leaps. I decided to refresh my resume and take the interview for McDonald's.

When I first saw the McDonald's job description on a PR listserv, the description left instructions to call for more information and questions. I called after 9:00 p.m., hoping to leave a message (I was unsure if I was ready to speak to a real, live human about a new job), but a woman picked up the phone.

We had a nice chat, after which Dana, the woman on the other end of the line, asked me to please apply. When I hesitated, she said, "I can't interview you if you don't apply." I smiled. The person who got this position would work closely with her, and she was excited to meet me.

While you're setting your course, make sure to do the following:

- **Read your resume.** Reflect on what you've accomplished and what you are most proud of. Whether it's tracking your daily gratitude or journaling about big moments, capturing how you feel helps you remember that it happened and it was important.

- **What would make you feel better?** Often when people ask how they can help, we don't have an answer. Think ahead about what friends and family can do to support you while you are under pressure. Get creative! I once asked a friend to plan a vacation for me to force me to go, because I knew I wouldn't do it for myself.

- **Inspire yourself with positive relationships and mentors.** At your lowest points, look for someone who can give you a boost when you are too tired to think creatively about the next step. If you can study one success story, you can find the strength to keep going.

- **There are no standard answers.** No mentor had my job, but they each had pieces of it. Whether it was an experience or an industry, look for people relevant to your current or future situation to help guide you.

- **Consider a breadth of experience.** When you think about how you want to invest your time, consider who you trust to lead you. What is important for your mentor, sponsor, or activist to know about you? I've benefited from mentors of different races, colors, and backgrounds—each time it's made me more understanding of a new perspective. Explaining my triggers, thoughts, and reactions to a mentor and seeking advice on how to manage myself prepared me for the workforce and to engage people with different lived experiences. My mentors taught me to view critiques with curiosity to build my self-awareness, and creating feedback loops helps me prioritize where I need to spend more time.

> Evolution is about moving from where you are
> to where you want to be. You can't do it alone.
> Pay attention to who is trying to guide you to the next level.

I was only a few weeks into my career at McDonald's when I met Mr. Don Thompson. He was the chief operating officer of the U.S. business at the time, and Lisa, his communications person, was taking a field role for more experience; she offered me an opportunity to advance by letting me fill in for her. It changed my career.

During a trip to taste test the Angus Burger and Sweet Tea in Pittsburgh, Mr. Thompson asked me what I wanted to do and who I wanted to be professionally. Without hesitation, I told him I wanted to be an executive speechwriter and I wanted to write for him. After that, we worked together for eight years; we wrote speeches for 30,000 people and developed partnerships with the Congressional Black Caucus, the National Urban League, and the NAACP. During that time, his authentic, spiritual, and diversity-focused leadership style was rewarded, and he was promoted again and again.

On August 24, 2006 at 9:00 a.m., I wrote the message where Mr. Thompson accepted the position of president of McDonald's USA. "I want to thank you for your ongoing, tireless commitment to our business—the McFamily is as strong as ever, and I am humbled to be asked to lead McDonald's USA into the future. Together we will build on the strong foundation already established. McDonald's is not a company built on just one person. We have created an amazing pipeline of talent and strong succession planning for growth within the company."

Along with Mr. Thompson, the company promoted the first Latinx chief operating officer for McDonald's Corporation and the first woman to lead the company as executive vice president and chief operating officer of McDonald's USA. It was a huge moment to see as a young professional and a woman of color. As I wrote Mr. Thompson's internal voicemail in the war room with the communications team, I realized we were witnessing history.

One of the world's greatest brands was empowering diverse talent to lead the future of food. We had forty consecutive months of positive comparable sales in the US, with consistent year-over-year margin growth. We were leading turnarounds in Canada and Mexico with a modernized menu and reimagining programs for the restaurants. We had a national campaign for the Dollar Menu, and were aligning owner/operators, suppliers, and staff around the McDonald's Plan to Win strategy. We were making evolutionary shifts that would permanently change the face of the company.

This was the start of a turnaround story four years in the making, one that saw us striving to improve the brand and the business. Our strategy was to be "better, not just bigger," and our global Plan to Win was creating business momentum around the world. I was twenty-five, writing the speeches delivered to investors, franchisees, employees, and the board of directors.

It helps to communicate the scale of this job if I explain the US arm of McDonald's and its position in the overall company. At the time the US was the company's largest business segment, responsible for the operation of more than 13,700 restaurants—nearly 45 percent of the more than 31,000 McDonald's restaurants worldwide. In 2006, the US business generated a sales increase of 5.2 percent, our fourth consecutive year of comparable sales growth. US revenues reached a record $7.5 billion, up 7 percent over the prior year. In addition, the US contributed 60 percent of the company's 2006 operating income. Overall, four years after the launch of Plan to Win, the US's performance was outstanding.

But we weren't done. The question we were asked most often was, how will you sustain your growth? In every speech I wrote, we had to address that question. This strategy started with the most important building block of any company's evolution: our people, me included.

Mr. Thompson would tell me during rehearsals how we had to include more real, deserving individuals—recognize managers instead of publishing stock photography. He wanted the world to see who was behind the greatest sales and customer service, and reward them. He taught me to give flowers to people while they are living, not just on their graves when they've passed. It was his way of telling me to honor life. He wanted to elevate his fellow employees, to lift them up rather than break them down.

He told me to always take opportunities, and he believed in me. As a division president, Mr. Thompson helped lead the crucial reorganization of the US business for unprecedented growth, and as he moved through executive vice president and chief operating officer for the US business, I was able to watch and learn from him every step of the way.

Watching Don lead with humanity helped me see how I could help this massive brand invest in the communities we served and make a real difference to our customers. From providing sanitation education in Asia to sports team celebrations in Canada, McDonald's was more than cheeseburgers to me. I watched Mr. Thompson lead McDonald's to rebound the U.S. business by focusing on core menu items and leveraging the strength of our community, franchisees, suppliers, and employees to meet our customer's expectations. He made me believe that winning meant doing our best for our customers, our brand and our investors.

During this golden age of having the most diverse team in the history of one of the world's biggest corporations, we were facing big issues—a shrinking workforce and increasing competition for labor. Our restaurants were dependent on immigrant labor in the midst of three federal minimum wage increases. We had twenty-three states introducing bills in 2007 requiring health care, and the fight for workers' benefits was heating up. Mr. Thompson was focused on our people, and launched a strategy to ensure all the employers in our system had access to subsidies to help with insurance for their employees. My job was to make sure the facts were right, my boss was prepared, and there were no surprises.

It was an exhausting time, but I came through it over-whelmingly for the better. The public edited my work. People still tell me about what lines I should've cut or what they thought Don should've said. I learned to balance the criticism and lobbying in a big company with what the CEO thinks matters, and my work during this historic regime meant that as I evolved as a leader and a person, I made an impact that was bigger than I could have ever imagined.

It's Down to You

You are the master of your fate and the captain of your soul. It's up to you to determine what you are willing to accept. Even as I had placed that call to apply for the McDonald's position all those years ago, I had been talking myself out of going for the job. *What if the next job isn't better? What if it's not worth it?* These frantic what-ifs, if I'd followed their nervous cautions, could have prevented me from taking a huge leap forward in my life.

In my career at McDonald's, I had the incredible op-portunity to meet President Barack Obama while he was a senator for the great state of Illinois. I almost missed the meeting being too into doing my job, but when I made it into the room I was rewarded with life-changing advice. Never say you can't do something until you try. When someone asks you if you can do something, you should always say that you will try. Always try.

Instead of getting distracted by all the things that could happen or all the ways I could potentially fail, I had to visualize and define the one thing I wanted to achieve. Then I had to ask: *Am I limiting myself in my current situation? Can I be doing more?*

During one particularly difficult project, I was traveling to some regional offices outside of the United States to conduct focus groups and identify some stories we could use for an upcoming global campaign to showcase our dynamic employees.

With each trip I learned how to introduce myself with authority, establish credibility, and explain my definition of success outside of the operations of the office. By clearly communicating my role, my reporting structure, and my definition of success, I gained credibility with global market leaders.

In all of the focus groups I conducted, the executive team had a similar appreciation for their top performers: no matter what was asked of them, the best performers had the confidence to try. During one leadership review, the senior executive shared that he valued employees that acted like a dolphin: ambitious, focused, good at repetitive tasks, yet free spirited. He shared that dolphins are the smartest animal in the ocean, and yet they know the value of putting in work and respecting leadership. Their ideal candidate was receptive to company standards and willing to fit in to a general company culture. While individuality is important, employers also want the reliability of knowing a task will be performed without fail. In each case when an employee is given more responsibility, they are also given a greater opportunity to fail.

Seeing each step as an opportunity to play on a bigger stage with bigger risk can motivate or paralyze a new leader; having the support to understand the importance of taking on the task despite the outcome helped me to build my confidence. I did projects no one had done before with fewer resources, less time, and better outcomes because I was willing to look at my situation differently. Instead of seeing these tasks as barriers to your success, view them as opportunities to build trust. Volunteer for huge team projects with vague scopes and small budgets because they'll be a chance for you to lead and build deep relationships with your superiors.

Devolving

Sometimes, you might go through the entire TRIBE process only to realize that instead of needing to change your position, you might just need a break. That's what happened to Nathan.

At one time, Nathan was a high-performing employee. He cared about his team and was socially engaged at work, and as a result, he advanced rapidly up the career ladder. But by the time we worked together, things had changed. He spent his time fooling around and never seemed to actually accomplish anything tangible. Coworkers loved him, but that was because of his charisma, not anything he achieved or brought to the team.

The reason for his laziness and busy work was a problem that we all struggle with from time to time: he was burned out. It happens to everyone, especially after years and years of work. But Nathan didn't know how to deal with it. Rather than recognizing that he needed to take a break in order to re-center himself and get back in touch with his goals and priorities, he just gave up entirely.

He didn't realize how, in doing this, he hurt his team. He was a distraction. His tasks in projects became dead weight. He gave others an excuse to become stagnant themselves. All the while, he waited for . . . what? For the universe to somehow remove his burnout. That's not to say that he didn't care about his team—he loved them. He just couldn't realize that what he was doing was actively harming them.

Nathan could never tell me what his role was in winning. Instead he avoided leading calls, managed to skip meetings due to conflicts, and passed work to other departments or team members. When I asked for status updates on his project he could never describe what they added to the bottom line. There was never a business value to his work—he didn't understand the business or how we made money. He viewed his role as a *traffic* manager, not a people manager. The job he really did was to avoid doing any work.

Everyone knew what was happening, but no one could stop it. I threw him lifeline after lifeline, but he didn't want to be saved. When I spoke to another team leader about Nathan, I said to them, "When I ask Nathan to describe his role, he struggles to share how he leads or directs work. Can you send me testimonials from your direct reports on how our team supports your department goals—in particular Nathan's leadership? Then we can be fair and hear from everyone's teams before we make any more talent decisions."

Within a few weeks of the meeting between me and the other team leader, Nathan's coworkers were empowered to share their frustration. They recognized the same themes in his work. One by one they found the courage to talk about his stagnant work style.

I was as transparent with Nathan as I could be about his performance. I gave him clear projects to work on and set new expectations. He would explain to me why my projects weren't important, tell me that they were a waste of time, and then spend hours working on pointless personal projects instead.

Eventually, he was terminated. When that time came, he wasn't surprised.

It's important to recognize that burnout doesn't go away on its own. If you are suffering from burnout, you need to come up with an individual action plan that changes your day-to-day routine. The only way to help others be better is for you to be better yourself. It's the business equivalent of putting on your own oxygen mask before you help anyone else with theirs. People will only respect the opinion of a high-performing employee, not of someone who is merely socially engaged. Your performance matters.

The rut Nathan had established for himself presented him with no way forward. He didn't *want* to become a better version of himself or fulfill any sort of goal. He just wanted to work as little as possible and hope that somehow he'd escape notice. Ultimately, the person he was hurting most was himself.

Looking to the Future

I hate the question *Where do you see yourself in five years?* To me, it feels like it's a backwards question. With the TRIBE process, you instead create your life goals by figuring out what makes you happy and which skills will give you the options for additional income in the future. Then you decide the appropriate career strategy for you.

Rather than spouting off something unplanned, ask how the company's plans will be impacted by hiring and organizational structure. No matter your age or experience, you want to be clear about your future and the expectation for your role. Will you have direct reports? Will your title change? Will you have access to additional resources to develop your external brand? Clarifying your manager's support for your goals and the alignment with expectations for your role is an early indicator of your communication synergy and trust. Look for the job with a clear scope of work and understanding of your priorities and time frame.

Your degree of success is determined by access, accountability, and ambition. Life is not a meritocracy, you are going to need a plan to promote yourself. Assume you can be great, and make a living and pursue a career you love. Visualize what life could look like if you focused on your goals.

ACTIVITY 6: NEVER STOP EVOLVING

"They tried to bury us,
they did not know we were seeds."
—*Mexican proverb*

In this final activity, you are creating a new reality. Take time to review all of your responses to the activities in the book. How does what you have done this week compare to your statements you wrote down during your week of possibilities? What changes have you implemented and what is the impact? What are you willing to do differently?

Evolution is about learning how to change and getting comfortable with the process. As you think about where you are headed, your resources, innovation, and beliefs proactively address the fears that can keep us stuck, challenge our vision and unconsciously hold us back.

It's time to focus on your future and speak positively about what you want in your life.

STEP 1:

Journal about the questions below:

- What is the best way for me to communicate my intentionality to others?
- How can I get support to overcome my challenges?
- Do I have any relationships that have been damaged by limited beliefs? How can I repair them?
- Have I made people better for working with me/knowing me?
- What are my intentions for personal growth?
- Is the way I am living my life aligned with my developmental goals?

STEP 2:

As you set your intentions, remember to write clear and defined statements. Intentions should be active and positive: "I will become this," not "This will happen to me." For example, "Health and wealth are flowing towards me."

Use the examples of intentions following to write your own.

Support:

- I don't have to face challenges on my own. I have resources and relationships that will help me.
- Whenever I approach a problem, I will focus on every single thing I can bring against it—I will think creatively.
- The most important people in my life are those who are willing to help me get past obstacles. They are the relationships most worth cultivating.

Relationships:

- I know people from all walks of life. When I speak with them, I will endeavor to keep an open mind, regardless of my own beliefs.
- I am true to my word and contributing to my relationships.
- If I have damaged a relationship through an inability to change, I will reach out to the other person and try to understand their position.

Positive change:

- I am confident in my ability to make the world a better place.
- Whenever I interact with someone, it should be with

the intention of making us both better for having had the conversation.

- When I leave a place, it should be better than when I first arrived there.

Personal growth:
- I am a successful leader, and people want to work with me.
- I am complete and one with the universe.
- I recognize the places in which I need to evolve, and will work on shaping myself toward them.
- Every day in every way, I'm getting better.

Developmental goals:
- I am overcoming every obstacle that stands in my way.
- I am in love with the person I see in the mirror. My career challenges me and enables me to grow.
- My thoughts are positive and move me towards my vision.

Actions I will take:
1.
2.
3.

CONCLUSION

Love is the answer to everything in life.

If I could give you a flowchart that would help you make all the right moves in your journey, I would. God knows I could have used one myself. But that's not what TRIBE is all about. There's no one-size-fits-all set of instructions to ensure your success, nor is there a single definition of success. Life isn't a straight line, and when you get lost, pick this book up to remember why you got started down that path in the first place.

I hope you walk away from this book with a set of values and a commitment to prioritizing the things that truly matter and will do the most to help you grow to get where you want to be. I'm sure you've noticed by now that TRIBE isn't a magic wand or even a big secret. It's a collection of guidelines—markers to lead you down the path that will move you forward in a way that best fits your goals. It's a way of life—a philosophy of growth and evolution that will help you become the best version of yourself. Life is full of cycles and understanding where you are is half the challenge.

Many careers are made from small moments that only make sense in the rear view. Sometimes the most impactful aspects of your work seemed like nothing at the time. Tiny things built up over time define a life.

Every little step you take matters. Every moment of Time is one you can use or waste. Every Resource you encounter can form a part of your toolbox. Every Innovation you make can be a stepping stone on the way forward. Every Belief you honor can elevate others. And every moment of Evolution contributes to your legacy.

If you'd told me at the start of my career where I'd end up today, I wouldn't have believed you. When I began discovering the TRIBE process, I was a single woman dedicated to my work. I wore blinders in regards to my health, family, and personal goals. I was too focused on my job and I missed the opportunity to develop myself. But I am profoundly grateful for the journey that led me here. Through it, I found my purpose, my passion, my person; I shaped myself into who I am, all because I learned from others who reflected TRIBE in their own lives.

I revisited my experience and my TRIBE when I decided to end my marriage in early 2020. In the midst of COVID-19 lockdown I went through the difficult process of adapting to being a single parent to my two boys. As a writer, I felt stuck going through an experience I wasn't ready to share because I didn't know if it would work. The truth is, without a test, we don't get the confidence to know what we can achieve.

I believe you found this book because you are on the cusp of something that might be new for you and the fear is making you feel like you are stuck. Being stuck can feel like purgatory. You know that you don't want to be here, but because you don't have clarity about where you want to end up, you settle for where you are right now. The truth is, you are not stuck.

Read that again: YOU ARE NOT STUCK.

You are exactly where you WANT to be. Every day we hear miraculous stories of people who have overcome poverty and made a way without mentors, successful parents, or a stream of income they didn't create for themselves. So it's possible and it could be you. Getting Unstuck means deciding to get started.

Decide today that you will start making progress the way you'd like to, notice how your experience will begin to shift. Reading your responses and revisiting your vision will help you make the right decisions for your life and foster the support system to survive and then thrive.

Whatever you are healing from, you are worth your

time. Getting Unstuck is a long term process and a lifestyle. There are no shortcuts, only guides along the way.

I've found having a clear vision for what I want is my greatest motivation when life is hard. Even on my worst days, my family and my work were constant reminders that I was living my life on purpose. I continue to do what I love, helping increase the visibility of women of color. I hope by reading *Getting Unstuck* you can find the best solution for you and your life.

Still stuck? Here's what to do next:

1. *Look at your notes you took while doing those activities and answer the questions you skipped.*

Taking the time to listen to yourself and understand what you want is critical. Don't skip this step or you risk spending time on someone else's vision without developing your own.

Affirm yourself: I already have everything I need to be successful.

2. *Set a timeline for action.*

It's never too late to change your life. When we stop evolving, we die. It is normal to have an area of your life that you want to improve. Decide what's reasonable and pick three steps that will help you.

For example, if you realize you need to get an executive coach to help you clarify what you want and how you'll take action, your first step is to get clear on where you need help.

Career coaches can help you articulate your skills to position you for your next promotion or build a network in a new industry.

3. *What are you willing to do?*

Whatever you are facing, it will take intention and it will take time. Expect setbacks and celebrate them because you know what? PEOPLE WHO NEVER TRY, NEVER FAIL. And it takes failure to move forward. So shift your mindset to enjoy evolving into the next version of yourself. You deserve to enjoy rising up to the challenge in front of you.

How much time do you have to commit to changing the world? Likely reading this book took you a few hours. It took me months to write it and almost 40 years of lived experience to share my story. I invested the time starting in 2013 to journal because I knew it would help my potential clients start their journey even before we begin coaching. What are you working towards and do you know what it will take?

Affirm yourself: I trust the plan the universe has for me.

Here's the tough truth. You can always find reasons to avoid what's difficult in life. It's not easy to make more money, set boundaries, work multiple jobs or say no to things you used to do.

The good news is, you have the power to change your life when you reframe why you are stuck.

The other good news, there are people who can help you. I'm one of them. You are officially not alone.

What is the meaning in your current situation? Maybe your current employer has offered you access to a leadership development program, executive coaching, or asked you to lead an internal initiative that will help you raise your profile. Many organizations have budgets for leaders to hire outside coaches and enroll in opportunities that will help you be a better leader and employee. Now is the time to explain how your manager and team can support you and create an environment that will motivate you to contribute more of your special talents at work.

Get comfortable being uncomfortable and go out there! Get unstuck, return again and again to TRIBE, and become the person you were destined to be. It starts with you. Send me an email or a DM on social media if you need encouragement to put Getting Unstuck into action.

One last affirmation before I go:
I am here to help.

> "Until the lion learns to write,
> every story will glorify the hunter."
> —*African proverb*

ACKNOWLEDGMENTS

This book would not be possible without the sacrifice of every person, living and dead, who built a place where my dreams can come true. Thank you to my hometown of Minneapolis-St. Paul, Minnesota, and every person who still fights for the right for everyone to have access to education, housing, and the opportunity to pursue their definition of success.

To my ex-husband, thank you for creating the space in our lives and our home for this book to happen. To my sons, live your dreams! Whatever you want to do, I hope this book reminds you to make every moment count. Never let anyone tell you what you cannot do. Thank you to my parents, my sister, and brother—thank you for being you and letting me be me.

Thank you to Mr. Don Thompson and Mrs. Liz Thompson for including me in your family and supporting me inside and outside of work. To my courageous and inclusive mentor, Ms. Pat Harris, thank you for your time and always telling me the truth. And to all the McFamily and especially the people I am honored to call colleagues: Deanna Jevremov, Dana Dodzik, Lisa Magnuson, Susan Nelson, Richard Ellis, Shannelle Armstrong, Ben Stringfellow, Genevieve Howland, Heidi Barker, and Suzelle Tempero.

To everyone who ever hired me, believed in me, or sponsored me—thank you for changing my life for the better. To Miss Tonkin, Ms. Gloria Woods, Ms. Dena Randolph, and Ms. Autumn Adkins for showing me how to embrace my Black girl magic at Breck School. To my beloved Ms. Jean Perry and Ms. Paulette Porter, who hired me as a student life worker at Howard University, thank you for teaching me how to hustle and get things done.

Thank you to everyone who trusted my leadership and management skills at Verizon, Delaware Investments, Lincoln Financial Group, McDonald's Corporation, 3M, and Comcast NBCUniversal. I would like to especially thank the people who opened doors for me during my career in corporate America by hiring me starting with Mr. Walter English Jr., Ms. Mary Papamarkou, Ms. Yvonne Yancy, Mr. Steve Tompos, Mrs. Kim Price, Mr. Ian Hardgrove, Mr. Emmett Coleman, and Mrs. Charisse R. Lillie. To learn more about how you can advocate for women of color in leadership and connect with me, text UNSTUCK to 66866 or visit gettingunstuckguide.com.

Thank you, the mothers of the Jeremiah Program, for inspiring me to advance my career and family with this book. Thank you to the Wise Ink family for helping me achieve a lifelong goal and teaching me the value of a great publisher!

This book would not be possible without the generous support of the John S. and James L. Knight Foundation and the support of Mr. Jai Winston and Mrs. Phuong O'Neil for believing in me and the revitalization of the capital city of St. Paul, Minnesota.

ABOUT THE AUTHOR

If you want to be inspired by the impact you can have inside and outside corporate America, meet Meredith Leigh Moore. After leading brand and reputation communications for McDonald's, 3M, and Comcast, Meredith now creates opportunities for inclusion through programs and partnerships. As president of Leverette Weekes, Meredith helps corporations authentically connect with inclusive resources to support their leadership development goals, including advancing women in their organization. Based in the Twin Cities, Meredith teaches how to manage your career effectively incorporating mindfulness and mentors in *Getting Unstuck: A Guide to Moving Your Career Forward.* In addition to entrepreneurship, Meredith leads external communications for Cleveland Avenue venture capital firm and is a 2021 Black Venture Insitute Fellow.

After Meredith's career started in finance, she found herself writing for the chief operations officer of McDonald's USA. Meredith supported the most diverse senior leadership in the history of McDonald's, including the historic rise of the company's first African American CEO. During her time at the largest fast food restaurant in the world, Meredith led award-winning global initiatives and external brand engagement resulting in McDonald's recognition as a diversity leader and talent developer.

Meredith's journey through the ranks to become the youngest director at McDonald's is featured in *Successful Women Think Differently* by Valorie Burton and a variety of other publications, including *Diversity Woman* magazine. She has been recognized as one of *Ebony* magazine's Top 30 Young Leaders and is the youngest recipient of Howard University's Global Visionary Award. She has also been recognized by the *Minneapolis-St. Paul Business Journal*'s annual 40 Under 40 Awards.

An advocate for access to education, Meredith holds a bachelor's degree in journalism from Howard University and a master's of science in managerial communications from Northwestern University. She is a member of the International Coaching Federation and Public Relations Society of America. She shares her insights for Forbes. com readers as a member of the Forbes Coaching Council. Outside of work, Meredith is a trustee of the F. R. Bigelow Foundation and serves on the national governing board of Jeremiah Program. During her free time, she enjoys reading, playing basketball with her sons, and connecting with friends.

Meredith is divorced and raising her two sons to know they have the power to write their own definition of success.

CPSIA information can be obtained
at www.ICGtesting.com
Printed in the USA
BVHW072020120821
614310BV00002B/9